T0066762

Hurting Hearts Hurting World and Faith

Judith A. Graham

WestBow®
PRESS
A DIVISION OF THOMAS NELSON
& ZONDERVAN

Copyright © 2014 Judith Graham.

All rights reserved. No part of this book may be used or reproduced by any means, graphic, electronic, or mechanical, including photocopying, recording, taping or by any information storage retrieval system without the written permission of the publisher except in the case of brief quotations embodied in critical articles and reviews.

WestBow Press books may be ordered through booksellers or by contacting:

WestBow Press
A Division of Thomas Nelson & Zondervan
1663 Liberty Drive
Bloomington, IN 47403
www.westbowpress.com
1 (866) 928-1240

Because of the dynamic nature of the Internet, any web addresses or links contained in this book may have changed since publication and may no longer be valid. The views expressed in this work are solely those of the author and do not necessarily reflect the views of the publisher, and the publisher hereby disclaims any responsibility for them.

Any people depicted in stock imagery provided by Thinkstock are models, and such images are being used for illustrative purposes only. Certain stock imagery © Thinkstock.

ISBN: 978-1-4908-2689-9 (sc)
ISBN: 978-1-4908-2690-5 (e)

Library of Congress Control Number: 2014903095

Printed in the United States of America.

WestBow Press rev. date: 04/21/2014

I wish to thank Kent Pankratz, for helping me edit this book and my husband Glenn for his help and encouragement.

CHAPTER ONE

My Life as a Child

As a child growing up in the fifties, when spring began we would go on our occasional weekend car rides. My stepfather would drive, mother would be in the front, and my older sister - who was fourteen months older than me, would accompany me in the back seat. Going on car rides wasn't my favorite thing to do because I would get car sick quite often. I remember telling mother when I needed to get out of the car in a hurry to throw up on the side of the road - she told me that my face had a slightly green tint to it. I suppose she was right since I remember well the terrible nausea I went through because of the crooked roads dad would go on. Car rides to this day are still not my favorite thing to do. Talking for all of us in the car would be at a minimal because any noise my sister and I would make always upset dad. I don't remember my other older sister - who was nine years older - ever being on any of the rides with us, probably because she got car sick too. Also there was my older brother, who was rarely around because he was always getting in trouble with the law and spending most of his youth being locked up. I remember being afraid of him when he would be at home with us because he seemed like a stranger to me. He liked to pick on my sister and he thought being mean was funny. I remember seeing him grab her arm and twist the skin in two different ways to make it have a burning feeling, causing her skin to become red. I know a lot of his problems were caused by our biological father who was very abusive toward him. I never knew my real father because he was killed in a logging accident when I was six months old.

1

My half-brother didn't come into the family until several years later, when my mother remarried again.

My stepfather was the only father I had ever known and he had diabetes. This disease affects the whole body, including one's mental state. As I look back at the way he ate and how mother cooked. I can see how he was not eating properly enough to manage his health problem. I remember going to town with him when I was about eight years old in his black Ford pickup. We stopped at a grocery store and he bought a dozen maple bars. I ate one and he ate the rest in less than an hour. He was also somewhat abusive toward both of my sisters- and older brother, when he was around; especially when dad would lose his temper. Not so much with me because I was too afraid of getting into trouble. Because of this I was labeled the "favorite child" – "the good child" and was told I was spoiled. I don't remember any special treatment. In fact, I remember neglect and emotional abuse.

I remember one ride in particular where I was looking out of the car window at hills that looked as big as a mountain to a small girl's eyes. I can still feel the very strong longing to be with God and a desire to be in a happier place. It was my belief that if I could just climb to the top of the mountain I could touch the hand of God. These feelings were so real to a young girl's heart - such a desire to have and to be touched by God at such a young age. He planted faith in me which lay dormant for many years until He brought me into His heavenly family. Sometimes I feel that I wasted many years not serving God, but if I hadn't gone through what I went through as a child and through some of my adulthood, I would not have been able to write to help others in their struggles. He let me go through my storms so I could serve Him better. After all, His timing is different than ours and His wisdom is beyond ours, and to fulfill God's heavenly plan is more important than any of life's burdens we have to go through.

We were created with the need to be loved by God and loved by others, whether they are believes or not. Our hearts were meant to love others. This need for love that God put in us comes directly from Heaven. It is who we are. We were created in the image of God. God is love **(1 John 4:8 NKJ) He who does not love does not know God, for God is love.** He gave us the ability to show love if one was raised with love. To those who were not life can be a very difficult, lonely, and a heavy burden.

I was raised without hearing the words "I love you.", and don't remember ever getting any hugs from my mother because she was suffering from depression. This wasn't something I understood or realized until many, many years later. Her emotional and physical abuse must have started when she was a baby. She told me at the age of four she had to pack water to heat on the wood stove. She stood on an apple box to reach the sink to wash dishes. Her mother, my grandmother, was quick to raise her hand and slap her across the face if she felt she needed it. She thought that her mother must have been the meanest woman in the world. It wasn't until many years later before my mother realized that maybe there was something wrong with her mother, and the reason why she treating her badly was because she was also treated the same way. When Mother grew into a teenager she had had enough and finally told her mother to never slap her across the face again. Mother told me that was the last day she felt her mother's hand hit her face.

Because my mother was raised this way it was carried over to her children. There was probably a desire for wanting her children to have a better life and being treated better, but her struggles in her mind made it difficult. Since she was hit across the face, the one thing she said she hated, mother never did this to us. You can see there was a possibility that she was trying to do better, but there was an occasional willow switch across the bare legs to get us moving and to do what she wanted us to do.

I believe because she was never shown love or taught how to love others, she couldn't show her children love. She was very withdrawn keeping all her feelings inside and never spoke up for us when we needed her support. If she got really frustrated at something, usually because of one of us kids she would curse, but only used the "D" word, telling me once that she had the right to curse now and then because of pure frustration. Maybe she was always at her breaking point. Like a spring in a toy that was always wound to tight. You just never know when it will finally break and then give up.

All of us kids were taught how to be depressed because we were raised around it - how to have low self-esteem and not enjoy life. As I look back at my dear mother there must have been more going on with her besides depression. If we had anything that brought us enjoyment she would always make some kind of excuse to remove it from our lives. There were a few times when I rescued a toy from the garbage can that was next to the fence in our yard. I don't know if she ever found out about my attempt of keeping my toy with me.

When I was about six years old mother made me a foot-long wooden sword. One of the neighbor boys wanted to see it so I handed it to him, and he quickly ran away with the sword. I remember feeling a little shocked that he took it from me. I went home and told Mother what had happened and her response was, "That's what you get for sharing." It quickly became my fault and sharing became a wrong thing to do.

I also learned not to share things with Mother because it was always my fault that things happened the way they did. I never told her when I went to the carnival that was in town and that I was touched by a man that work with the carnival and it made me feel very uncomfortable and scared. It was a long and frightening ride because he was watching and smiling at me every time I flew around, and when it stopped I quickly untied the rope and jumped down - running as fast as I could to my home where I kept the terrible secret. I felt very guilty because I knew it was my fault and I had done something wrong. I know now if I did tell my mother she would have done nothing about it, but I am sure she would have just told me not to go back over there. There was a good possibility that I never went to another carnival that came to town, but I do not remember.

She must have suffered terribly with her mind in a constant darkness, with no one to help her and not knowing where to get help for herself, or maybe not even wanting any. I felt that she spent all of her life waiting to die. That is why when she developed cancer - she never sought help. She suffered needlessly. A doctor could have helped her and made her more comfortable in her last days. It was hard for me to hear her say, "If I had a gun, I would end this right now". Just what was I suppose too say to that? I vowed, then and there, that I would never let my children see me suffer in this way. I would seek help if I became ill, but I had learned to block out reality and even if she was sick and dying I couldn't really see it because of the wall I had built around myself. I don't want to give the impression that Mother was the worst mother in the world. There were smiles once in a while in her darkness, and I am so thankful that there are a few good memories that are still with me. I still miss her. She did believe in God, but because of all her sadness her faith could not grow to be fruitful for the Lord.

My mother's mother had a very hard life. How much of the story I am about to tell you is accurate or whether it is even true I cannot say, but it was told to me. When she was young teenage girl she was traded to a very old man for a team of horses, which we know would lead to a probability of abuse and rape. She escaped by pushing him under a train and killing him. His brother found out what she had done and came after her with a shotgun, intent on ending her life. She ran to the house, grabbed her belongings and ran out the back to keep her life. She was always moving from one town to the next so the neighbors would not get to know her because she was afraid of being found out. She could not go back home and she most likely had no desire to, anyway. For my great grandparents to trade their daughter like that meant that they were not very good parents. Indeed, it was a horrible thing to do to my grandmother if it was true.

I do know that she was a superstitious woman - telling me if you drop a spoon you were going to get a big disappointment, if you dropped a fork a woman was coming to visit, if you dropped a knife you were going to have a male visitor - things of that sort. I also remember when she was dying she kept looking at her fingernails, which she believed would show her when death was approaching. My mother told me that she had a terrible fear of going to hell for what she had done, but at that time in my life I had no idea what had happened to her. I never heard or knew of any repenting prayer for her sins. I can see now why my grandmother treated her daughter poorly. The things she went through put a lot of scars on her heart, spirit, and soul, which carried over into my mother's life. I do wonder how my great, great grandparents treated their sons and daughters. My, what a vicious cycle of pain families pass on to the next generation of children!

As I look back on my life and how I struggled with depression, anxiety and low self-esteem - how I carried all that garbage for so many years not realizing it - I am surprised of how well I have done over the years. I wasn't the greatest mother to my two girls. I had a very hard time letting them get close to me and the words I love you were very hard for me to say, but as I got older and they got older the words became easier for me to say. Now that they are grown the "I love you" words fly all over the place, and my two wonderful grandchildren have been taught to say these three magical words as well. Some of the curse on this family has been taken away because of one person's changed heart which was touched by our loving Creator. My depression and anxiety still haunt me once in a while, but I try not to let it control me. I tell myself every day that I am a child of God and this child before Him is His joy. Keeping focused on my loving Father in heaven helps me a great deal, and I am looking forward to be in heaven where all this will be taken away someday.

CHAPTER TWO

The Words We Speak

We are affected by the words spoken by those around us. These words will build one up or tear one down, bring encouragement, or bring discouragement. They will fill you with fear or the courage to try something new. The Bible says in **(James 3:1-12)** that the tongue is a little member of the body, but can cause many problems. It can boast great things. It can give praise to God and curse your neighbor at the same time. Like a forest fire it can be started with just one small match. A fight can begin with few words. When you continue to call a child stupid they can become angry and discouraged. They will feel rejected if always told to go away or to go to their room. Our actions are reinforced by what words we put with it.

As an example, let's say you yell at your child to leave you alone because you are too busy to talk, or do not want to be bothered by them. When we yell with negative words this can make a child have low self-esteem. It tells them they aren't important to you and what you are doing at that moment is more important. They will feel rejected. How do you think this child would begin to act because of what we continue to do and say? I believe that they would start misbehaving and taking it out on their younger sibling - if they have any. Their grades at school could be affected and their anger inside could be carried over to the playground. They could start fights with their class mates and the more they get into fights, the more the parent will yell at them - or they will become a little girl or boy that fades away into the background that no one can see. These children are vulnerable to experimenting with drugs and alcohol as a way to try to escape and fill their emptiness they carry inside. Young girls that did not receive comfort from their parents can turn to immature young men for comfort not even realizing what they are doing. Their actions can bring on unwanted pregnancies or diseases.

The hooks are being buried deep into the hearts of our children. They are learning that fighting, yelling, and cursing are the way a family should act. Since they only see one side of the story they will think it is normal. A young child may also want to cling to you more because they want your approval, love, and reassurance that they are important to you. When a child is raised with no one to turn to when they need to have some reassurance or comfort when needed, they will retreat to their bedroom to feel secure, making a place where they can keep all their secrets. Just may be, when they are all alone in their room, they learn to think only of themselves - like how they can make themselves happy or how to protect their wounded heart. By building a wall around their world they have custom made just for them. They are not taught to think about others, causing the heart in the child to be selfish. This results in a selfish person that does not know how to reach out to others and feels more comfortable being alone as an adult.

(Proverbs 22:6 NKJ) says, **"Train a child in the way he should go, and when he is old he will not depart from it."** How, and what, we teach our children will stay with them the rest of their lives. If it is with negativity then they will be a negative person and this will then be taught to their children. However, if we were to teach our children how God says we are to - love and care for one another, even those we do not know - then there is hope that they will become loving and generous adults. That would be the best thing we could do for our children and the world. In **(Colossians 3:21 NKJ)** it says, **"Fathers, do not provoke your children, lest they become discouraged."** When we yell and curse at our children we are teaching them to do the same. When we emotionally neglect them and show no love or encouragement, they will be filled with emptiness - always looking for what they did not receive as a child with those around them as adults. There is more trouble in the making there because one would probably be drawn to someone that had the same negative upbringing from their parents. What kind of relationship do you think this would be creating if this was so?

Generation, after generation families carry excess baggage to the next. The luggage of abuse, anger, hopelessness, depression, mental illness (which, I feel can be a fifty percent learned behavior, and fifty present hereditary,) drugs, alcoholism, and how one learns to treats others. This is a very hurting world. It consumes the soul, breaks the spirit inside, and causes one to feel empty. We suffer needlessly for things that could have been avoided if one were to follow the wisdom from God. I truly believe that there is hope for change for all who surrender their lives over to God. We need to slide over to the passenger side and let God do the driving. I became tired of taking the wrong road a long time ago, but I must admit sometimes I still put my hand on the steering wheel and try to drive (and my Good Shepherd, Jesus, lets me drive into the ditch or take the wrong road to remind me that I need to trust Him to drive this car of life.) We must realize that God is asking us to do our very best and He will do the rest.

CHAPTER THREE

Our Need for God

The need for God's love to be in the hearts of all people upon this world is clear. There is so much need that it seems overwhelming to the mind. We don't have to be like this, but people have become souls that don't care anymore - having no belief in the Creator. Many are walking around like empty shells filled with darkness and no hope. Many are being taught that it is just the way people are. Yes indeed, there are many that feel this way, but why do they choose to be this way? The god of this world, Satan, wants all to live in his darkness. His darkness hardens the heart, creating no love for mankind, no forgiveness, selfishness, and no belief in the loving Father in Heaven. It is his goal to destroy as many as he can before God destroys him and all the angels that followed him.

The anger that lives in the heart is a negative emotion that produces other negative thoughts. Each negative thought will feed upon the other, keeping the fire burning as long as there is fuel to feed it. Hatred grows from anger and it is capable of keeping one locked in a dark room with no way out. It will surround the heart of the individual like a cage, keeping these feelings in. As hatred and anger branch out from the soul it will produce a selfish person with the attitude of "I don't care, it is all about me." They will think of themselves first, with no forgiveness to the one who caused pain in their life. If impulsive thinking comes into play, caused by the heat of the moment, it can lead to loss of life and loss of freedom. This constant negativity can result in illness, physical or mental, because it suppresses the immune system and grieves the

Holy Spirit. The worst thing that could happen is the loss of another soul – to feel separation from God – because this is what will happen if one cannot step away from anger and hate, letting forgiveness in. There are only two choices waiting for everyone: Heaven or Hell. You might say it is God's way, or the highway that leads away from Him eternally. There are no other choices.

Anger and hatred can be in everyone, but how can one have these feeling without keeping them daily in the heart? We were created in the image of God and He hates sin. So then should we. He is angry with men for the sins they do. If you believe this, then you should be living a Godly life that will keep God's anger from coming upon us, and keep His hand of protection with us. To be angry with an injustice is not wrong. To hate the sins of men is not wrong. If the anger and hatred is focused on a wrong then it is justified, but one must not let this build up in the heart and mind. Then these feelings will replace the gentleness of God's love. Your focus on God will be clouded with this world because your feelings will blind your eyes to your own inner actions. All injustices need to be placed into the hands of God for Him to take care of. We must trust in Him and believe that He knows what is best for us as individuals.

God's word clearly says that vengeance is His.

> **(Romans 12:17-21 NKJ) Repay no one evil for evil. Have regard for good things in the sight of all men. If it is possible, as much as depends on you, live peaceably with all men. Beloved, do not avenge yourself, but rather give place to wrath; for it is written, "Vengeance is Mine, I will repay," says the Lord. Therefore, if your enemy hungers feed him; if he thirsts, give him drink: for in doing so you will heap coals of fire on his head** (you will soften his angry heart). **Do not be overcome by evil, but overcome evil with good.**

We need to step aside and let God's strength take care of it. He will make it right. If we try to be the judge and jury we might find ourselves getting in too deep to get out without it coming back at us and causing problems for ourselves. For every action there has to be a reaction, whether negative or positive, and God will not let the sins of men go unpunished.

Abuse that is done to another is a self-centered lust that fills the heart completely, whether it is sexual, physical, or mental. It is the worst thing one can do. It produces many souls that are filled with helplessness. The heart is broken and the spirit becomes weak. These sinful acts will cause mental problems that will become heavy burdens throughout one's life and carry over to the next generation. The trust that is broken cannot be given back to the abused person without the abuser seeking help and forgiveness from the ones they hurt. It will take a long time to forgive or trust the ones who brought pain into their lives. For some the hurt is so deep that it will take the touch of God's healing hand and His love to be able to forgive them and trust anyone again.

There are many that walk around living their daily lives with no hope for their future. They see only this one life in front of them. To them there is nothing else out there. To me there is more evidence to the contrary – that this world that we live on is filled with such beauty and detail that it could not be here just by chance. People tend to look past what is around them and focus only on their own desires. Self-satisfaction is what they only seek. They fail to look up to see the beautiful rainbow or glorious sunset. We as humans upon this earth forget that we are suspended out in space circling the powerful sun. This beautiful blue ball is God's creation, but there are those who believe it all started with a big bang theory. If it was so it was God who flipped the switch. I refuse to accept that life began in a mud puddle. Someone had to make the mud puddle first. We need our Creator more than anyone could ever imagine. We need His love to live in our daily lives. I need Him more than the beating of my heart and every breath I take into my God-given lungs.

CHAPTER FOUR

Idolatry in the Heart of Man

Hope is a gift from God. When one has hope for their future then the heart becomes lighter and life is worthwhile. We need to have hope. We were meant to look up to the living Creator with the understanding of why we are here. We were created to love and worship Him because He loved us first. Time is precious, and it is passing by very quickly. Many are losing the opportunity of walking with the Spirit of God - refusing to acknowledge His existence. Maybe it is because they don't want to see their own vulnerability or accept their responsibility of their own actions - seeing themselves as sinners under the eyes of God. To see this is to accept that He does exist and that His Son Jesus came to save us from ourselves to walk among sinful man.

> **(Exodus 20:1-6 NKJ) And God spoke all these words, saying: "I am the Lord your God, who brought you out of the land of Egypt, out of the house of bondage. You shall have no other gods before me. You shall not make for yourself a carved image - any likeness of anything that is in heaven above, or that is in the earth beneath, or that is in the water under the earth; you shall not bow down to them nor serve them. For I, the Lord your God, am a jealous God, visiting the iniquity of the fathers upon the children to the**

third and fourth generations of those who hate me, but show mercy to thousands, to those who love me, and keep my commandments.

What exactly is sin? The definition in the dictionary is this: an act that breaks a religious or moral law. If you were to open the Bible (which I hope you do), you can read the laws that were written by the hand of God. They are the Ten Commandments, which were given to show what sin is. In **Exodus 20:3-17** it begins with the first law, telling all not to have any other gods before Him - revealing His sovereignty as Lord and Creator. He gave us this command because He deserves and desires our full attention. He knows all of our weaknesses and longs to be loved by His children. The second law tells us that we are not to make any image to worship, admire, serve, or bow down to - whether it is paper, canvas, wood, stone, glass, gold, silver, ceramic or mud. Nothing is to be made so that you can bow down to it. India, which is called the land of a many gods, is a good example. Watching a documentary about this I saw a man sitting among what he worshiped - rats.

These rodents were crawling all over him. His body was thin and his eyes were filled with emptiness and had a glassy look. The ones that worship these rats believed that drinking the water that the rats urinated in was a blessing to them. They also brought food to them daily. If one were to get bitten it is a blessing, even if many deaths are from the diseases that these rodents carry in their bites.

In God's wisdom He tells all who worship idols that they are doing it in vain. This belief will destroy the body and soul, keeping one blinded from the truth. Can a man-made idol help in any way? Can it save the body or soul? Can it answer prayers? Can it take you to a better place that God has for those who follow Jesus Christ to heaven? It cannot do any of these things, so what good does it do for the soul of those who worship rodents, or worship a Buddha statue, or any other idol? We are told to show respect for those who worship false gods and their religious beliefs. I believe this is true, but we are also told to reach out to those who do this - to save souls with the good news about Jesus Christ, our Lord and King.

The futility of idols - the pointlessness of worshiping things that come from the mind and heart of men - is clear. The Bible speaks of idols and how God is against this sin. In **(Psalms 106:34-35 NKJ)** it tells how disobedience to God and worshiping idols led His people into self-made hardships and how He showed mercy to His peoples,

> "They did not destroy the peoples, concerning whom the Lord had commanded them, but mingled with the Gentiles and learned their works; to serve their idols, which became a snare to them. They sacrificed their sons, and their daughters to demons, and shed innocent blood. The blood of their sons and daughters, whom they sacrificed to the idols of Canaan; and the land, was polluted with blood. Therefore the wrath of the Lord was kindled against His people. Many times He delivered them; but, they rebelled in their counsel, and were brought low for their iniquity. Nevertheless He regarded their affliction when He heard their cry. And for their sake He remembered His covenant and relented according to the multitude of His mercies."

(Psalms 115:4-8 NKJ) says,

> "Their idols are silver and gold, the work of men's hands. They have mouths, but they do not speak; eyes they have, but they do not see; they have ears, but they do not hear; noses they have, but they do not smell; they have hands, but they do not handle; feet they have, but they do not walk; nor do they mutter through their throat. Those who make them are like them; so is everyone who trusts in them."

We cannot, and should not trust in something that gathers dust and needs to be kept cleaned. Many give offerings to appease the god of their choice - like food and flowers - and you know that the food would rot because it wasn't eaten and the flowers would wither away for lack of water. There are many others things that fall under the category of idolatry - anything that you put ahead of God. Anything that is more important than Him is idolatry. Pride is a form of idolatry because you are thinking of yourself more than one ought to. Self-importance can make you look down on others. Putting yourself on top of a pedestal will cause you to come crashing down some day, and pride is one thing that our loving Father hates. **(Proverbs 6:16-19 NKJ)** says,

> **"These six things the Lord hates, yes seven are abomination to Him; a proud look, a lying tongue, hands that shed innocent blood, a heart that devises wicked plans, feet that are swift in running to evil, a false witness who speaks lies, and one who sows discord among brethren."**

Then there is food, material things, and position in society. Money is a big one because you will make it your security instead in the Lord being your security, and wealth will put a false wall of protection around you.

Our need for the Father in heaven is great. We need to count on Him for all things. Yes He does want us to prosper, not just financially but spiritually, and for us to love Him with all our heart. **(Matthew 6:33 KJ)** says, **"Seek ye first the Kingdom of God, and all these things shall be added to thee."** The key to prosperity in one's life is just that - put God first. Turn from the things that will keep your thoughts too busy to think of Him, and make time to talk to Him through prayer in your daily lives. We can be poor as a church mouse but rich with God's love - that is Heaven's prosperity. However, we must be still before Him so we can hear that small voice that leads to fulfill Heaven's will. When our thoughts get too busy we can miss His leading through the Holy Spirit presence, and miss out on the plans He made for us before we were born into this world. Keeping the line of communication from you up to Heaven taunt will keep your faith strong inside.

CHAPTER FIVE

How Holy is the Name of God?

(Exodus 20:7) says, "You shall not take the name of the Lord your God in vain, for the Lord will not hold him guiltless who takes His name in vain."

The name of God, Jehovah, is holy and eternal **(Genesis 1:1 NKJ) "In the beginning God created the heavens and the earth."** He is the Creator of the universe. He is God. So what is in His name?

Almighty God, "El-Shaddai" **(Joel 1:15),** tells of His power. He is powerful enough to fulfill all our needs and to keep His promises. Lord (Jehovah) is the great "I am" **(Exodus 3:4)** - the One who is forever and has sovereignty over all the earth and universe. He is Jehovah "Rophe" **(Exodus 15:1-26 NKJ)**, the One that heals. For the ones that follow him nothing is too hurtful, or is too big, or too small that He cannot heal. He is the One who see all things, that includes what you have in your heart. He is "El Roi" **(Genesis 16:1-16).** Our loving God cares for all deeply and wants to be in our daily lives. He is Lord "Adonai" **(Isaiah 6:1-13)** - master of His creation, including you. We all have a choice to follow Him or turn away. He will not force you. It must be of free will when one surrenders the heart. He is the good Shepherd "Jehovah-Roni" **(Ezekiel 34:1-31)**, that will lead with loving kindness His children that He cares for. He is "Jehovah-Saboath" **(Zachariah 8:1-23)** who is above all things and reigns with righteous judgment, and shows compassion. He is Alpha and Omega **(Revelation 22:13)**, the beginning and the end, and there is no other like Him!

There are three that abide in the truth: The Father, the Son Jesus, and the Holy Spirit - and all these are one. To comprehend how all three could be one is beyond what we can understand. When Jesus came from the beauty of Heaven to walk upon this earth to bring the good news He brought many names that revealed His Father. He was the light of the world **(John 8:12)** and was the word of God **(Revelation 19:13)**. These two names are telling all that He is the light in the darkness of the world that revealed the sins of men bringing the truth from heaven. He came to be the Savior of God's children **(1 John 4:14)** and Messiah **(John 1:41)** to lead us to the path of life and away from eternal destruction.

He came to be the Lamb of God **(John 1:29–Revelation 22:1)** to be a sacrifice for our salvation. This Lamb was without blemish - there was no sin in His heart or mind, and only He is worthy to be called the Lamb of God. He became the Chosen One of God **(Luke 23:35)** to bring the Bread of Life **(John 6:35)**. He is Immanuel **(Matthew 1:23)**, which means God with us. He is Jesus our Lord, our Judge, our King of Glory, the Anointed one, Messiah the Prince **(Daniel 9:25)**. He is our Advocate **(1 John 2:1)** - the one who speaks to God for our behalf revealing our worth. As Chief Shepherd **(1 Peter 5:4)** he is above all leaders and He is the Christ. **(Matthew 16:16)** The Holy Spirit, God's power, was sent to be with us when Jesus rose from His grave to go back to His Father. It was promised that we would not be left alone **(John 14: 16-18)**. The Holy Spirit is here to be our Comforter and the one who guides us through our lives to fulfill the Father's will.

The third law given by God says we are not to take the Lords name in vain. To say His name in a way that degrades Him or makes Him seem useless is breaking this law, and for those who have no true belief in His existence He may seem unreachable. Some can be hiding the fear of the truth in their thoughts, or are in complete denial. He is everywhere. He is in every breath we take. **(Genesis 1-2 NKJ)** says, **"The spirit of God hovered over the waters"**. I am sure there are those who like to rub their non-believing, empty, arrogant hearts at the face of God and laugh at those who believe in

Jesus, the Son of God. Let them laugh, but their laughter will turn into complete fear when our Eternal Judge calls out their name and their name isn't in The Book of Life. Our loving Father in heaven deserves our respect and all worship be given to Him only. To have someone use His name so fruitlessly is not right and I have hatred for the words they speak against my Father in heaven. I know it offends God, so it offends me, also.

The love of God is everlasting for His children and He lovingly calls to the hearts of those He chooses. He is so rich with mercy that He is willing to forgive the most horrific sin. He wants all to bring their burdens to Him so He can lift them away from their shoulders. This is done because He cares greatly for us as individuals. He offers this amazing love to this world, meaning everyone who walks upon this earth. His name is the most Holy name there ever could be. When we fear of the Lord by believing in His power (a power that is above all things) and humbling our self before Him, it is the beginning of wisdom. The Bible says in **(Proverbs 9:10 NKJ), "The fear of the Lord is the beginning of wisdom, and the knowledge of the Holy One is understanding."** That fear should mean that you respect Him with reverence because you know He is the only true living God, and remembering He could take your life away from you if He so desires to do so. Whether you live or die is always in the hands of God. In **(Acts 5:3-5, 10 NKJ)**, one can read how our lives are in His hands:

> **"But a certain man named Ananias, with Sapphira his wife, sold a possession. And kept back part of the proceeds, his wife also was aware of it, and brought a certain part and laid it at the apostles' feet. But Peter said, "Ananias why has Satan filled your heart to lie to the Holy Spirit and kept back a part of the price of the land for yourself? While it remained, was it not your own? And after it was sold, was it not in your control? Why have you conceived this thing in the heart? You have not lied to men but to God?" Then Ananias, hearing these words, fell down**

19

and breathed his last.—then immediately she fell down at his feet and breathed her last."

God is there, therefore His power is real. Those who do not believe will be brought to their knees before Almighty God, because of their shame and sins. This question should be asked when we hear the words that rejects God,

"What if you are wrong?"

Why would anyone use His holy name in vain, for He loves everyone equally - a love that is without waver? This love can carry one through the toughest storms, and when you make it through another storm in this life your trust in Him will grow a little more, bringing you closer to the Father in Heaven. His is beautiful because He glows with love. This love is so perfect that we cannot truly understand what a perfect love would be like, but to me a perfect love would be forgiving us of our sins despite all of our carnal minds and weaknesses as individuals. Remembering that we are here for but a moment and looking past our flaws with merciful eyes and a heart filled with grace. Jesus was meant to be our predestination for the atonement for our sins and blotting out the sins of all mankind - to be the salvation that will save us from eternal damnation. He gives a promise of eternal peace for those who willingly love the Lord with all their hearts and offers to all a new life that is paid in full. Jesus has taken away the power of sin and death that hovered over mankind. This is what true love is. Forever shall we be with the Lord.

We need to give honor where honor is do, praise where praising is do, and show respect to God's sovereignty as Creator of all the universe. He is the great **"I Am"**. **"I am...** the One who can save you." **"I am...** the One who loves you." **"I am...** the One who created you." **"I am...** the only One who can forgive you when you come before me. Your sins will be forgotten when you confess them in prayer to me". **"I am...** the One that will keep my covenant because of you."

CHAPTER SIX

A Time to Rest

(Exodus 20:8–11 NKJ): "Remember the Sabbath day, to keep it holy. Six days you shall labor and do all your work, but the seventh day is the Sabbath of the Lord your God. In it you shall do no work; you, nor your son, nor your daughter, nor your male servant, nor your female servant, nor your cattle, nor your stranger who is within your gates. For in six days the Lord made the heavens and the earth, the sea, and all that is in them, and rested on the seventh day. Therefore the Lord blessed the Sabbath day and hallowed it."

In the wisdom of God there is a reason why He wants us to keep His laws. He knows if we weren't given rules to live by our lives would become a terrible mess, and that is why people bring trouble into their lives. They don't believe in the laws given by God, or they have never been told about them. The law of keeping the Sabbath holy is there to show that one needs to rest from their daily work. It is there to remind all that He is God and that He wants us to live by His moral laws. With rest we can be rejuvenated physically and spiritually. The body can become ill when we work constantly without rest. We can also miss out on enjoying life that is God given.

Keeping the Sabbath and resting from one's work gives respect and honor to God. It is a blessing to have time away from our daily work.

That doesn't mean not to move or do any work at all. If you have babies and very young children they need to be taken care of, and the family needs to have their meals cooked for them then it is what one must do. One doesn't have to finish painting the house or plow the back forty. It is lawful though to do good things on the Sabbath, such as taking care of the elderly in nursing homes and working in a hospital with the ill patients. These are things that have to be done. In **(Mark 3:3-4 NKJ)** it says, **"And He (Jesus) said to the man who had a withered hand, "Step forward." Then He said to them, "Is it lawful on the Sabbath to good or do evil, to save life or to kill?"** Jesus came to free us from religious laws that men wrote and to show us the truth from Heaven.

The Sabbath is the seventh day of the week and is from sunset to sunset. It is a twenty-four hour day. This is the time we are commanded to rest and draw closer to the Creator. As I look at many churches having their church services on Sunday, the first day of the week, I ask how this can be correct because God's law says the seventh day not the first day, which would be Saturday not Sunday. If we were to look at man's work week it will usually start on Monday, but we need to look at creation week, which starts on Sunday. The name of the day is not important. They could be named one through seven and would not make any difference. God's written law is His law. Does anyone have the right to change it?

Sometimes I wonder about the Sabbath keeping on a certain day. It is when I look at a well-known evangelist who kept Sunday, the first day of the week, and how he did great things for God - how he brought many souls into the kingdom of God with the strength of the Holy Spirit. He was faithful in doing the work that the Lord led him to do and still desires to give God honor in his old age. I guess we need to just ask for guidance throughout our lives, trusting Him to lead the way with this prayer upon the heart. Even though I speak my thoughts about the Sabbath I do not believe that whoever keeps Sunday as their Sabbath will not receive the gift of eternal life. Going to church will not get you into heaven. It is what is in the heart that will get you there, as we hold onto a belief that Jesus is the Son of God, and believing through His death life will be given to all who choose to believe, and by follow the footsteps of the Lamb of God.

CHAPTER SEVEN

Give Honor and Respect

(Exodus 20:12 NKJ): "Honor your father and your mother, that you days may be long upon the land which the Lord your God is giving to you."

I had what you call "shirttail cousin's" living next to my family home. These children were abused by their parents. I once saw the father kick his son so hard in the backside that it lifted him off the ground. The boy walked off limping and his dad laughed at what he had done. I can still see him as he turned and looked at me with such empty laughter. He had shown with this action that there was no carrying for or love for his son. I came over to play once as they were finishing up their lunch. I saw the father reached over and take the meat off of one of his children's plates because he wanted it. My mother use to give the kids water to drink with the hose through the fence in the summer time because their mother would lock them out of the house. She thought that eating her chocolates and reading her romance books was more important than her children, and I don't want to bring to mind what else they were doing to their children behind closed doors and how I was putting myself in harm's way by being there. I saw the results of this abuse when they grew up. This abuse was so ingrained in their children that it was the same way they treated their children. Due to the abuse they did toward all of their children they both died alone of cancer. The children now grown wanted nothing to with their parents. I consider parents who treat their gifts from God this way not parents at all, but dictators – abusers who control with fear.

God says in the fifth commandment that we are to honor our father and mother, and our days will be long on the land which the Lord our God has given us. Honor has to be earned. Respect must also be earned. Our children are our greatest treasure, but when these precious jewels become tarnished with the darkness of anger and abuse they cannot shine to give God glory. How can any child show respect to a parent that is abusive? How can they love others if they are not shown love? How can they have a forgiving heart without having someone to be a good role model? There is no way they can show love to anyone, including them. They may say the words I love you, but can those words be really coming from the heart? How we live our lives before our children will mold our children's lives. If a person smokes and does a lot of drinking, then there is a good chance that their children will do the same. If they hear cursing all the time, then they will learn to use those words when they are angry or joking around. I know that there are parents out there that are trying their best to raising their children right, but sometimes a child will choose the wrong path anyway. This world has many things out there that will influence their decision making. We need to teach our children right from wrong. It is important for their future and well- being.

Once I took classes on teaching and was told by the instructor that when children say they are sorry there is no way that they really mean it. I believe that this man was wrong and I told him that I was in total disagreement with his statement. I have always taught my grandchildren to say they were sorry when they did something wrong to another. When my granddaughter was three years old she jumped on the back of her older brother and hurt him. He began to cry and without me saying a word she went over to him and gave him a hug with the words "I am sorry brother." Children need to know how to treat others, and I believe they can understand the words "I love you" and "I am sorry" more than adults realize. Our children won't have empty hearts when they are shown kindness and love. Even if you give your dog a pat on the head to show your love for them they will respond with affectionate lick to the nose and a wagging tail.

God wants everyone to treat others with respect and love, which will show His influence upon our lives. We were meant to love Him and to love others. The need for God to be in every home is so great that it would take a miracle from Him for this to happen in this world, and that sounds like Heaven to me. There are many homes that hide terrible secrets that would overwhelm one with a gentle heart. It is like one little candle in the hand of someone with the love of the Lord standing in front of a fifty foot black wall of darkness. The need for Jesus in all our lives is our greatest need. He is the only One that can heal broken bodies and broken hearts. The promise of peace and joy in Heaven is waiting for those who choose to believe and turn from this sinful world. They will see this world be changed because of God's wonderful and amazing love, and the memory of all this darkness will never come to mind. This should fill our hearts and minds with hope of Heavens eternal love and beauty.

CHAPTER EIGHT

Having Respect for Life

(Exodus 20:13 NKJ), "You shall not murder."

The sixth commandment from God is that you shall not murder. This act takes away the humanity from the heart of the one that commits this sin. Compassion and caring for your fellow neighbor is not there, and the heart is filled with a demon of darkness. It is especially horrific when it involves a child. You may wonder, as I often do, how someone can do such an act. When one begins to think of a sin the seed has been planted. The more a person thinks of this sin, the more it will grow into the act itself. They have given into the temptation of the darkness of this sin, but before I go any further on this subject I must bring God's word in to show how we are to think. We all must see that every person has their own field of life to plant good seeds or plant bad seeds. Do we want a field that is bountiful, or do we want a field that is nothing but destructive weeds? In **(Galatians 6:7-8 NKJ)** it says, **"Do not be deceived, God is not mocked; for whatever a man sows, that he will reap. For he who sows to his flesh (evil desires) will of the flesh reap corruption, but who sows to the Spirit (doing God's will) will of the Spirit reap everlasting life."** Our thinking can be our downfall. We are to meditate on good things and have pleasant thoughts. In **(Philippians 4:8 NKJ)** it says, **"Finally, brethren, whatever things are true, whatever things are noble, whatever things are just, whatever things are pure, whatever things are lovely, whatever things are of good report,**

if there is any virtue and if anything praiseworthy-meditate on these things." Giving into sinful thoughts will destroy one's life and other lives and destroy the soul. The paradise of Heaven will never be seen.

The god of this world has kicked into high gear because he knows his time is short. Look at the madness of the world that is shown daily in the news. This angry and hurting world is filled with no hope. Many see there is no way out - there is nothing else. It is a dog-eat-dog world. Can you imagine how much worse this world would be if no one believed in God's word or if no one lived with God's laws in their heart? The Bible say there is a time for war and in war people die, but fighting against the madness of this world is different than sneaking into a home to fulfill the evilness of the heart.

There are many reasons behind killing: jealousy, hate, greed, envy, lust, vengeance and anger. All these negative feeling from someone comes from this world. Jealousy in a relationship means there is no trust in a marriage. If you cannot trust your spouse, then there could be a reason for this or it is just your imagination. Dwelling on this can lead to a crime of passion and a marriage that becomes broken. When murder comes into the heart you have let the devil into your thoughts, and when he gets control of your actions you have lost your anchor with the Lord. With every temptation He will make a way out. In **1 (Corinthians 10:13 NKJ)** it says, **"no temptation has over taken you except such is common to man; but God is faithful, who will not allow you to be tempted beyond what you are able, but with the temptation will also make a way of escape, that you may be able to bear it."** This is a promise from our Creator. He is telling us that He will let all this madness in the hearts of men only go so far, but we must choose right from wrong by making the choice of stepping away from sinful temptations that can destroy our life.

The hand of God is upon all who believe and follow Jesus Christ our Lord. He is by the sides of those who grieve a loss, who cry for strength, and who ask for wisdom and need His presence in their daily lives. In the Bible it tells of a man of faith, Job. This man was blessed by God because of his faithfulness and obedience to Him. God's hand of protection was upon this man of faith. Satan complained how He had

27

His hand of protection around him all the time – how does He know that he would not turn from his faith if the protection was not there? So God lifted His hand away from him that kept hardships away letting Satan to step in, but he was not allowed to touch him. The flood of loss came and had attacks on his health, but he never turned from God. With his mouth he cursed the day he was born, but he never turned his anger toward God.

> **(Job 5:8-9,17): "But as for me, I would seek God, and to God I would commit my cause-Who does great things, and unsearchable, marvelous things without number. Behold, happy is the man whom God corrects; therefore do not despise the chastening of the Almighty."**

Hate and anger were in his heart and he could have turned this toward God, but he did not. It could have destroyed his love for God but Job refused to do this.

Hate is a very strong word. It can eat at the soul like cancer eats away at the body. It will keep you from forgiving, and it will keep your faith in God from growing and maturing. It will keep God's hand of protection away from you. Hate and anger can result in action. Hatred for America is in many countries. It is powerful and is ingrained into the people that live there. Anger turned to hate, and hate turned to action. That is why all those people died on 9/11. Hate and anger are very good companions because they are always together.

Greed and envy are two more companions that seem to stick together. It seems like someone always wants something someone else has. They have no desire to work hard to receive the harvest from their labors. The wisdom of God's word says that we are to be content with what we have, and if seek the kingdom of God first and all our needs will be met. **(Matthew 6:33 NKJ)** says, **"Seek ye first the Kingdom of God, and His righteousness, and all these things shall be added unto you."** Just how much more of a giving world would this be if one would have this living within their mind and heart? When one has lust in the heart it could be something other than sex.

Lust also can be greed and a vengeful desire. If you live to eat, not eat to live, then food has become your lust and idol. You eat more to try to fill this desire and empty space in you.

Following God's wisdom in His word is the only way to get through this world. We are all His creation no matter how horrible a person could be. We are capable of showing both kindness and unspeakable cruelty. We can forgive or hate with a force that can consume the soul. We can make the choice of a sinful life, or turn from the sins that are destroying men, women, and children. The choices that one makes not only affect the individual, but the ones that are around them.

CHAPTER NINE

Is Marriage God-Given?

(Exodus 20:14 NKJ): "You shall not commit adultery."

(Genesis 2:21-22 NKJ): "And the Lord caused a deep sleep to fall on Adam, and he slept; and He took one of his ribs, and closed up the flesh in its place. Then the rib which the Lord God had taken from the man He made into a woman, and He brought her to him." From the beginning men and women were meant to be together. God created the first marriage by joining the Adam and Eve together. They became one.

Marriage was given by God as a gift. Were we meant to have a companion that would give support and comfort through the tough times and to share joyful times and happiness together, but many are making light of the seriousness of marriage and enter into this union with expectations of a utopia – every day will be perfect and there will be no problems to deal with. They think it will be a fairytale marriage – living happily ever after – just like a movie, but that just isn't so. There is an old country song that says that she never promises a garden of roses, or lots of sunshine, and life without rain. So true is this. Good or bad, life happens. We have to deal with it and hopefully one will have support from your spouse, but how many run from the marriage when things become difficult?

When one desires to climb over the vows you took to get to the other side of the fence, you may find the same kind of grass and weeds you had on your side growing on the other side. You can run from the problems in the marriage but you cannot run from the problems that are inside of you. When you leave they will come with you. The fact is, when problems come up in the relationship between a man and woman it just can't be a one-sided thing. Life is harder for some than others, but we need to remember that no one is without flaws. If we could just look past the little stuff that bugs us about our husband or wife then we can remember how much we loved them on the wedding day. Then the union will stay together and not be broken.

Our hearts and bodies are here to give God glory. We cannot give our Creator the respect and honor He deserves when we mistreat the gift of marriage and do not respect our spouse. If we love them as God's word says we need to be doing, then why would one give into the lust of the heart because of wondering eyes? All are His creation and all are under His watchful eyes. If one believes they are doing their misdeeds without anyone knowing they are mistaken because God sees and will remember every detail in one's life.

When, a person climbs into bed with someone other than their wife or husband it is the beginning of the end of one's marriage. To think that it is not that big of a deal is a way to justify the sin. It is when all lying shall begin. There is an old saying that goes "Oh, what a web we weave when we first start to deceive," and the web will grow larger and eventually you will be caught in your own web of lies. When you do there is no running from this because it is exposed to the truth, and what you should have treasured may be lost forever. If there are children involved these hearts will be broken and become filled with anger, with the question of why don't you love Mommy or Daddy anymore.

The family unit is being destroyed before our very eyes. Marriage has become an outdated antique. To hear that someone is celebrating their fiftieth or seventieth anniversary is a wonderful thing to hear. What God has made is never wrong. It is the wisdom of this world that is taking over - a wisdom that is filled with flaws. When God says in His

Ten Commandment, "You shall not commit adultery", there is a reason for this law. It shows that His wisdom is far above ours and this rule was given to keep us out of trouble. We are a bunch of little children that are running around getting in all kinds of trouble. We need His guidance to be corrected by the Father in Heaven - to be humbled and feel shame for our misdeeds. Yes He is our Father, our Creator, and He knows what is best for each of us. He is our greatest need for this hurting and angry world.

CHAPTER TEN

Greed in the Heart

(Exodus 20:15 NKJ): "You shall not steal."

When one takes something that does not belong to them, they are breaking two commandments from God at the same time. They first covet something, and then they take it for themselves. We need to be satisfied with what we have and we are to be generous with what we have, as well. We are to give from the heart and not hold back our giving because of worry and fear of filling our own needs. God says we need to trust Him to fulfill our needs and desires. This will bring peace to the heart when we put our trust in Him. When we fret because we always want what the other person has, turmoil fills the heart and mind. When you receive that coveted object you will turn and see something else and start the process all over again. We are trying to satisfy the needs of the heart, but what we are truly doing is feeding the greed that lives in the heart.

Those who steal can do it quietly without someone seeing, or pull out a weapon and take it by force. They lie to get what they want. They come and cry on the shoulder with a very sad story. They get up in front of people and milk them until they run dry. After all, God wants all to have their hearts desire doesn't He? However, not every desire is for the good and not every desire is God given.

There is nothing wrong to want money to get out of debt. There is nothing wrong with a desire to be blessed financially to be able to help others. It is when we love money more than God - It is the reason why one gets pulled into this world and becomes anchored into the wrong foundation. This is a crumbing world that has a weak foundation. It will not go on forever, and I thank the Lord for this. Who in their right mind would want this madness to go on forever?

When one steals they have no trust in God to provide their needs or no desire to have the Lord in their lives. Most likely no true belief in the Father in Heaven either. They are giving into the lusts of this world. We need to see the difference between wants and needs. We need food, air and water, clean clothes, a bed to sleep in, transportation, and a safe home to live in. We need to see the things that God gives daily as a blessing and not use them for bad. We need to open our eyes and hearts to the reality of our greatest need, God. If you were to look into the mirror, what do you see? Do you see a person you would like to meet? Do you see someone with a generous heart? Or do you see someone that you do not trust or a person out of control? Whatever we are and whoever we are, we are all before the eyes of God. Our choices we make are determined by what lives in the heart. If we take what does not belong to us we are following the god of this world, and we are on a path that leads to destruction.

CHAPTER ELEVEN

Think Before Speaking

(Exodus 20:16 NKJ): "You shall not bear false witness against your neighbor."

As a child I played a game where we would whisper something in one ear and each child would whisper in another until it got back to the first child who started it. Every time it would be different. It was always funny to hear what it would end up to be, but when it comes to adults and their lies it isn't so funny. It is no longer a game. Lies can tear apart families and break the trust between a husband and wife. Lying can get you into trouble with the law and your work place. The gossip's tongue can start a lie that spreads like a wild fire. It can destroy someone's reputation.

So is there really such a thing as a little white lie – just a little fib can't hurt anyone and nobody will ever find out – after all it is for the best anyway, right? Whose best are we talking about? Isn't a lie just a lie and nothing else? Whether we tell a so called little lie or a big one they are equally the same. Just what does one consider a white lie to be, and why would they put with the word lie the color white? White symbolizes purity and cleanliness – a lie doesn't seem so pure or clean to me. Trying to cover it up with words or excuses won't change what it is. Maybe it is like having an old picket fence that is in need of a lot of repair. There are split rails, holes and rotten wood, so you decide to paint it white to make it look better. You step back and see how much better it looks, but under that new look it is still the fence that is rotten and needs to be replaced. You cannot change what a lie is with a few flowery words to make it better.

However, being totally truthful to everyone around you can hurt feelings and making one look like they do not to have any sensitivity toward someone else's feelings. We do not have to blurt out the truth to someone and tell what you think at all times. There is a couple of old saying that go, think before speaking, and loose lips sink ships. **(Proverbs 17:28 NKJ)** says, **"even a fool, when he holds his peace, is counted wise: and he that shuts his lips is esteemed a man of understanding."**

Have you heard some of these little lies before? "Oh, yeah, that makes sense." (When you didn't understand any of it), "It wasn't me!" (Saving yourself), "No officer…I had no idea that sign was there." (Hoping not to get a ticket), "Yes, he was with me last night." (To protect someone), "Oh yes, that dress looks good on you." (Thinking that it doesn't do a thing for her), "No thanks, I just ate." (Knowing how bad a cook they are, with your stomach growling), and the list goes on. In court we swear to tell the truth and nothing but the truth, but can one live their lives this way? Can you be a truthful and honest person without stepping on some ones toes and feelings? I feel that we can but we just need to choose our words wisely when we speak to others.

The Bible says there are many sins that do not lead to death. **(1 John 5:16-17 NKJ): "If anyone sees his brother sinning a sin which does not lead to death, he will ask, and He will give him life for those who commit sin not leading to death. I do not say that he should pray for that. All unrighteousness is sin, and there is sin not leading to death."**

So why do you think God says we are not to bear false witness against one another? It is because His wisdom is telling us that it will bring trouble upon the one that lies and cause pain for the one that is lied about. There is no one that has never told a lie. All are guilty of this. Thank goodness and Heaven above that we have a loving God who is willing to forgive our misdeeds.

CHAPTER TWELVE

Be Content with What You Have

(Exodus 20:17 NKJ): "You shall not covet your neighbor's house; you shall not covet your neighbor's wife (or husband); nor his male servant, nor his female servant, nor his ox, nor his donkey, nor anything else that is your neighbor's."

I have always thought that this is the most broken of all the laws God gave us to live by. Coveting that fills the heart can be very persuasive with the slightest thought. Envy and jealousy can cloud the mind with thoughts that this is not fair. Why can't I have their life style? I deserve that fancy house and their money more than they do.

We came into this world with nothing and we will surely leave with nothing. There will be absolutely no way we will be able to take even one penny with us. All of your collection of stuff will be left behind for others to gather up for themselves. The treasures of this world cannot satisfy the inner need of the heart. The true treasure that one should seek is the treasures in Heaven. We need to remember the more things we collect for ourselves, that there will always be someone out there that would take it from you in a heartbeat; if they had a chance to do so.

Do you think that coveting could be the beginning of all sin? Do we covet before we commit adultery? Lust comes into the heart and the seeking eyes begin. Do we covet before we steal? By planning to take something that doesn't belong to you we do. Do we covet when one makes an idol? We seek to see our choice of god that we can serve and bow down to, whether it is a carved statue or material things. We are trying to fulfill the inner need of worship – the very thing that God put in each of His children. Do we covet when we lie by seeking to satisfy one's own glory because of the prideful heart? God's word says that pride is idolatry.

In the news we see how not honoring ones parent can lead to terrible choices – how two boys killed their parents for their money. They let greed into the heart. They let the god of this world control their thoughts and control their actions. They coveted, lied, murdered, and tried to steal. Each of our choices we make, whether good or bad, will eventually catch up with us, and it will either be punishment or a blessing. One may go to the grave without any punishment from the laws of man, but when one stands before our Lord and King, the eternal Judge, all will be revealed, and all sin will be exposed in His light. Then one will be the goat that he will send to His left that leads to eternal hell.

Can you not see now how important it is to acknowledge the need for God to live in the heart? To see our greatest need is Jesus Christ, the Son of God, and to have an anchor in Jesus, the rock of our Salvation. We are all like little children and we have lost our way. We have turned from the Creator with a prideful heart by turning to the things of this world to satisfy the soul. We need to be willing to let God change the person that we hide inside ourselves, the one that He knows all about. We need to let God be our guide throughout our daily lives so we can make the right decisions, and to remember to trust God and that He's in control. It is my prayer that God will call to the hearts and bring His lost children into His heavenly family.

CHAPTER THIRTEEN

Our Children

To stop the family curses we as parents must begin to look at what is in our hearts and dig deep into the soul to let go of all the things of the past. We must first confront the things we have been carrying around for too many years, the baggage that keeps us from moving forward, so the healing can begin in the hurting family. We need to be dedicated to our children. We should love them and teach them right from wrong, and have a desire for them to live up to their potential without pushing them too far. Living a Godly life before them and being a good example of someone that loves the Lord Jesus will give them a better chance to grow up to be wonderful children of God. Our children are gifts from God; therefore they should be treated with love and kindness. We need to protect them from harm and guide them to eternity with Jesus. How precious it is when they have their first belly laugh? What a wonderful thing to see. Their first attempt to walk will bring you an excitement to see their desire to move forward. When something goes bump in the night you run to them to give them security from the scary things, showing them that they will be okay, and what a joy it is to have a little baby wrapped up in a blanket held next to you. We need to admit when our children are getting on our last nerve. We need to reach out for help when our past is haunting us or controlling us, and not take it out on our children. These little ones have a longing inside to be loved - to be taught to live the right way and to grow up in a home that will give them wonderful memories, not memories of abuse or neglect.

What more can I say to this hurting and angry world but reach out to the loving Father in Heaven? He is there give comfort to the child inside - the child that was abandoned, neglected, and abused. There is hope in the promises given from Heaven. There is peace waiting for those who choose to believe and accept the love of Jesus Christ, our Lord and King. Would you reach out to Him today so you're hurting and angry heart can receive the healing power of God's love? If you do, then you can live up to your potential to give God glory. Don't wait until tomorrow because tomorrow may never come. May all glory, be given to God in Heaven.

Jesus

Is

Our

Greatest

Need

Our True Need

The need for our Lord is clear,
Every day of our lives and throughout eternity-
There shall be many times we shall fall
Before the feet of Jesus seeking His mercy-
We need to hang onto the Lord and never let go,
For He is our strength and King-
Never take our eyes off of Him, giving the heart,
Surrendering to Him with praising-
You may think that God has turned from you,
But it is you that has turned from Him-
It is when you let go the hand of Jesus,
You will let the darkness of this world come in-
Oh, what a wonderful Savior we have,
For He forgives all of our shortcomings-
He will welcome you back to His loving arms
And pour upon you eternal blessings.

My Hiding Place

I praise you God for seeing past
The weaknesses that is in me-
For being by my side always
And the forgiveness from thee-

You are my strength and greatest need
When temptation will come before me-
I will hold onto your promises with faith,
Looking forward to being set free-

For, you are my only true hiding place,
Under your wings I will be still-
There is no one greater than you Lord;
For my heart you did fill

Through my Burdens are heavy

When my burdens are heavy
And I try to carry it all alone-
Then I find it overpowering me;
Making me feel all alone-

Your gentle voice tugs at my heart,
To surrender it all to you-
Lord, sustain me through this storm,
As I remember your precious truth.

The Key

Help me shut the door of the past
Turning to the see the light from Heaven-
Help me look away from this darkness,
Remembering through Jesus I am forgiven-

Help me with your eternal strength
To turn the key and to lock this door-
Help me give the key to you Jesus,
There you will keep it forevermore-

Help me to be the Christian you saw,
Before this world was and I came to be,
And I will walk where you lead dear Lord,
Giving glory and honor to thee.

What must I do?

Believe in Me and Jesus my Son.
I sent Him to save you-
Love me with all your heart
And to love others, too-

Turn away from the sins of this world
That your mind and eyes see-
Walk in the footsteps of my Son
And this will set you free-

Do not worry about tomorrow,
For I am already there-
Keep your heart secured in Heaven,
With a belief that I care-

Trust in me for all your needs.
Stand still before my eyes-
Rejoice, because I truly love you
And I will not cut our ties.

Golden Threads

Open up my heart Lord
And pour your words in-
With golden threads of love
Sew peace within-

Pull them tight and secure
Them with a knot-
So your words of life will stay
And never be forgotten-

Gift upon the Cross

Don't throw away the gift that Jesus
Gave upon the cross-
This precious gift was given because of love
To save the lost-

Angels rejoiced at the death of the Lamb
It was the Fathers will-
For there are no tears in Heaven above,
God's holly plan will be fulfilled.

Sing in Your Storms

The storms of this world surround me,
But I am not tossed to and fro-
I stand upon the Rock, anchored in belief,
Standing in your love that I have known-

A song of praise overflows from the heart,
I will sing praises to your holy name-
Only through trust and true belief
Is there heavenly gain-

I turn to the wind to see it coming
To try to destroy my faith in you-
But nothing can separate me from your love,
Your power and wisdom carry me through-

When I feel that I can no longer hold on
I call to you, and you give me your peace-
Filling me once again with your strength,
Giving me more hope and my fears released-

Peace, be still is what I hear in my heart
And I feel you holding my hand-
This storm will soon pass, revealing the sun,
Once again, you lead me to your peaceful land.

Be still before God

I will fiercely search for my sheep,
The ones that have gone astray-
Whatever direction they are going
I will lead them my way-

I will walk into their darkness,
And bring them into the light-
Whatever it takes I shall do,
To point them to what is right-

I will heal hearts and bind their wounds,
Bringing them back home-
Whatever I touch I will bless to show them
They are not alone.

The Puzzle Piece

Jesus is the missing puzzle piece
That completes your picture of love-
The piece that will fill the void in your heart,
Given from above-

The place that longs to have hope and faith,
With peace as you live-
He holds the piece in His loving hand;
Waiting for you to turn to Him-

He will place it gently in your heart
And seal His promises within-
Writing your name in the Book of Life
To bring you home someday to live with Him.

A Letter to Mother

I want to tell you how I miss you so
And how my children have grown-

Of the grandchildren that God gave to me
And how wonderful they are to see-

When I look back on my life with you,
Oh, how that little child was so sad and blue-

Wondering why you never helped the one so insecure,
That needing your love and a young voice to be heard-

I did not know what your soul was going through,
Not understanding the darkness that was in you-

In your sadness your mind was filled with despair,
Filling my mind of thoughts that you didn't care-

Now I know there was no one around to help you
And I am so sorry that I wasn't there to help you, too-

God was there. Your mind would not let your faith grow,
But your sadness is no more, for God took you home this I know-

I forgive you dear Mother, for not fulfilling my inner needs.
I love you with all my heart; forgiveness has set me free-

Someday we will be reunited again in our home far away,
There we shall bask in God's love; forever will we stay.

The memories of all our sadness and tears will be no more,
When God willingly opens up Heaven's doors

If Only I Had Known

If only I had known that it was you Lord
Knocking at my door-
I would have answered and my emptiness
Would be no more-

If only I had seen what a mess my life
Was in before I knew you-
I would have turned to your calling
And received peace from you-

If only I had recognized the darkness
That was trying to destroy me-
I would have ran to your loving light,
So that I could be set free-

If only I had known how much you cherished
This sinner that is before you-
I would have accepted Jesus into my heart,
So I could be close to you.

The White Rose

I promise to give you a change
In your life and heart-
If you would follow my lead
And do your part-

I promise to make the white rose
Bloom just for you-
If you would but trust my guidance,
Believing in Heaven's truth-

I promise not to let you go through
More than what your heart can take-
If you but surrender your all to me,
Believing in my Sons name-

I promise to always walk with you
Through your trials each day-
If you would but hold my hand child
For my light will lead the way.

Guiding Light from Heaven

Now is the time for healing;
The time to turn from this world-
To walk with the guiding light from Heaven,
Receiving strength from the Lord

Peace for the Mind

I refuse to let me destroy me!
My thoughts shall be only of you-
I shall turn from all the darkness
And walk only in your truth-

Letting not madness enter the heart,
Nor confusion in the mind-
Lord, fill me with your strength
Then, peace I will find.

Blessed are those who believe

Blessed are those who walk not with
The sins of this world-
For their joy is with the Lord above
And drinking in His holy word-

They shall be like the trees with roots
Secured by the living waters-
Bringing fruit in its time with strength
And shall never whither-

The wicked shall not be triumphant,
Nor escape God's judgment of man-
Their sins will be before the Lord and King,
With their fate resting in His hands-

For the Lord rewards the righteous heart,
Those who believe in Him-
But the ungodly will be sent away,
Because of their darkness within

Honoring my mother with fond memories

*Honor your father and mother,
that your days may be long upon
the land which the Lord your God
is giving you.*

Exodus 20:12

Winter Wonderland

The winter is long so silent and white;
The moon makes diamonds of frost at night-

The squirrels are snuggled all warm in their beds;
Children slide down the hill on their sleds-

The breath they can see on the chilly air,
While they laugh and tumble, with nary a care-

Oh, the winter is long, silent and white,
But the flowers will bloom when the sun shines bright-

The diamonds will melt and flow to the sea,
Then return next winter to shine for me.

Painters Dream

Who can paint the moan of the wind in the top of a tall tree?
Or the trill of the Meadow Lark, or the hum of the busy bee-

The flash of the trout in a mountain stream,
Or the call of a goose and a cougar's scream-

The roll of thunder of a summer's storm,
Or the bawl of cattle on a lonely farm-

The howl of the wolf on a moonlit night,
Or the whisper of owl wings near silent in flight-

These things are for the ear and not for the eye,
Or the brush of a painter; such as I

Death of a Monarch

A tall old pine tree stood high on the hill,
It had survived summer's heat and winters chill-

It had watched the fight of birds overhead,
And sheltered a deer as it sought a bed-

Heard the chatter of squirrels as they cut off its cones,
Then carried them away to their winter homes-

Became a lookout for a hunting hawk,
Now shivered, as it listened to men and their talk-

So far it had escaped the bite of the steel-
The ring of the ax and the winding reel-

It seemed the old tree now had to go,
What would become of it, it really couldn't know-

Perhaps it would become a ship at sea
And sail the ocean wild and free-

Or a house, or a bridge, or some kind of wood,
The old tree shivered in the place where it stood-

But wise old Mother Nature had a far better plan,
Out whiting the intents of this thing called man-

She sent a great storm and lightning did flash,
The old tree died; to earth it did crash-

It lies there still to this day;
The grand old monarch has gone nature's way.

Written by Ruby Clark (Surface- Beamer)

Faith

If faith were to be measured; what length would it be?
Would it be as tall a mountain or deep as the sea?
If faith were to be seen; what would one see?
Would it be the love of God; coming from you and me?

If faith were to be held; what amount would be there?
Would it be heavy or light when carried to heavens stairs?
If faith would be given; who would draw you near?
Would you believe it with no doubts and see it clear?

If faith were a gift, would you accept it from the Lord?
Would you believe that His truth is in His written word?
If faith came with eternity, would you fight for it with God's sword?
Would you fight for your soul, to live with the heavenly Lord?

CHAPTER ONE

Is your faith enough?

A person can claim they are a Christian even if they have no faith, but to be a true Christian their lives should show their faith in God and be a reflection of Jesus in their daily lives. If we only go through the motion of religion with no faith, then we are not Christian at all, but empty shells like the others in this world that are blinded by lies.

Should one be satisfied with just faith? If we believed in God and believe that Jesus is His Son, we do well, but would that be enough? Okay, it's enough, I believe, therefore I am saved. I don't have to do or, worry about all of that other stuff, but should we be satisfied with God placed on the back burner of our life? Keeping our faith just warm enough to say we are a Christian? What would have become of us if Jesus just stood there and not moved forward to do His Fathers will? Not to preach repentance and forgiveness for the sinners He came to save? Faith needs to be nurtured. It needs to be at the feet of Jesus daily. It must have action for it to grow because faith without works is dead.

> **(James 2:17-18 NKJ) Thus also faith by itself, if it does not have works, is dead. But someone will say, "You have faith and I have works." Show me your faith without your works and I will show my faith by my works... We need to be doing what the word of God say and not block it from**

going into the soul and heart, but be fruitful on the vine of faith.

(James 1:22 NKJ) But be doers of the word and not hearers only, deceiving yourselves.

We are to live by faith and not sight. This is what the Bible says, but what does this mean? It should mean to the individual that there is a trust in the Creator to be able to live by faith, for trust and faith are linked together. I have always told God that I understood this but a little picture now and then wouldn't hurt, either. Everyone needs encouragement once in a while from the Holy Spirit, to know that we are on the right track leading us to fulfill God's will. He will touch others to bring you the encouraging words that will lift your spirit up.

Picture it this way: when our faith gets low and we feel drained, it's like a car running low on fuel. It sputters and quits running. We are the cars that need to pull into the Holy Ghost filling station and be filled up once again with the love and strength of God. This battle we are in is a fight for our soul. We are being bombarded by the evilness of this world daily.

(Ephesians 6:12 NKJ) For, we do not wrestle against flesh and blood but against principalities; against powers; against the rulers of the darkness of this age; against spiritual host of wickedness in the heavenly places.

(Revelation 12:11 NKJ) "And they overcame him by the blood of the Lamb and by the word of their testimony and they did not love their lives to the death."

We must fill our hearts with our eternal hope Jesus, our Lord and King that came from Heaven. We must trust that He is in control and there are no accidents with God. Nothing can just be by chance, luck, or fate, because He does not make mistakes. These things are from this world and are not from Heaven. He will maneuver things around to fulfill His will; making even the non-believer walk the direction where He wants him to go to fulfill His will for the believer.

(Psalms 37:13 NKJ) The lord laughs at him, for He sees the day for him is coming.

There was a man, who was one of the rulers of the synagogue named Jairus **(Mark 5:22–23.)** He came to Jesus, fell at His feet and begged Him to come and heal his daughter that was at death's door. Jesus agreed and followed the man to his home. On the way a great multitude of people surrounded Him, pushing to get closer. Among the people was a woman who had a disease of the blood and had spent all that she had in the attempt to be healed by physicians, but was not cured. When she heard of the arrival of Jesus, who was known as a healer, she pushed through the crowd to get to Him. In her mind and heart she knew if she were to just touch the hem of His garment she would be healed **(Mark 5:25–29.)** The moment she touched His garment the healing power of Jesus came upon her and Jesus knew that His power went from Him. He had been touched by faith and asked, **"Who touched my clothes?" (Mark 5:30.)** This question confused His disciples, because He was being touched on all sides. Why did He ask this question? Since He is aware of all things; He is omniscient. Maybe it was because He wanted to be sure that the miracle that He planned was to be seen in the presence of others, which would bring glory to the Father in Heaven. His eyes searched out for this person. He saw the woman and when their eyes met she fell at the feet of Jesus with fear and told Him the reason why she touched Him. *His reply was,* **"Daughter, your faith has made you well. Go in peace, and be healed of your affliction, (Mark 5:34 NKJ)** but the child of the man Jairus had died.

Since his daughter was dead and there was nothing that could be done. They told them not to bother the teacher (Jesus) because it was too late, but Jesus had planned a miracle to show the power of His Father in Heaven and His authority as the Son of God. They arrived at the home of Jairus and He told them that the child was not dead but was sleeping. Of course He was ridiculed for such a statement, so He commanded the child to rise and she did, and to give her food. **(Mark 5:38–43.)** This left the ones that saw this miracle with amazement.

Did you notice that Jairus sought out Jesus and the woman did the same? She fell at the feet of Jesus because of faith and a willingness to move forward. Did you also notice He told her to go in peace after she was healed? That it was her faith combined with action that helped her to be healed. If she pushed up against Him without faith would she have received his healing?

Jesus is the great physician. He came to heal this world from the darkness of sin that is destroying lives and souls, wounding bodies, and breaking hearts. Open up your Bible and turn to **(John 3:16 NKJ)** in the New Testament and read what it says. **"For God so loved the world that He gave His only begotten Son. That whoever believes in Him should not perish but have everlasting life."** This verse is the heartbeat of His holy word. It is who God is. He is love, but this only shows a fraction of what is in the heart of God. What it shows is His great love for mankind. **"For God so loved the world"** that He sent His only Son Jesus Christ to be the Lamb of God to save His children. Jesus went willingly to the cross to suffer and die for our sins, misdeeds, and poor choices. This gift from God was, and is, the only way for us to be forgiven. THERE IS NO OTHER WAY! This precious gift was the greatest way to show His love for all men. Should not this bring great joy to the believer's heart? Should this not bring more trust in Him? Should we not give thanks daily for this gift that opens the doors of Heaven to those who repent of their sins and accept Jesus as their Savior? This should be all that we need to keep our eyes focused on Heaven and our hearts at the feet of Jesus upon the cross.

We are such weak vessels and are easily swayed by other people. Their smooth words can be very convincing. They love to prove that a Christian is wrong, because they believe that God is man-made. They are wrong, and they are standing with their pride of being an atheist before the eyes of God. Oh, how sad that is. Read this poem and it will reveal what came from my heart, with God leading my words.

Going out with the Tide

You believe there is no God-
But I say what if you are wrong?!
You are standing before your Creator
With no need of hearing heavenly songs-

Could, you not search your heart,
Letting go of your fear and pride?
Reaching into the soul to see any doubts;
Questioning the thoughts inside?

Living without God's love within the heart,
And flowing through your life;
You are swimming away from the safety of the shore,
Going out with the tide-

Not seeing the danger you face,
The judgment of body and soul that will be;
I pray that God will open up your blind eyes
So you can see His eternity.

Whether you believe or not Jesus, God's Son
Is coming to judge all-
This world will tremble! Lightning will strike!
And man's sinful world will fall!

Faith involves our willingness to follow through: to follow with the Holy Spirits leading. If God tells you to walk, then you must walk, but it is up to you to take the first step and then the next. True faith is what is needed, but when it comes to going blindly where men tell us to go then this is a mistake on our part. They can lead us over the cliff of eternal darkness, but following God and trusting Him to be our guide through this life with obedience to Him is what we must do. To trust that He has plans for each of us, even if one cannot see what is coming next, one must believe that God has everything in control and that He can work out the details. **(Philippians 1:6 NKJ)** says, **"being confident of this very thing, that He who begun a good work in you will complete it until the day of Jesus Christ.** Even though Jesus was speaking to His disciples I think this verse can be applied to our lives today. When God touches the heart of an individual to do something, as He touched the disciples, He will fulfill His will for that individual. It is then that we will become another light that shines into this world of darkness, and will be until and beyond the great day of Jesus Christ. **(Acts 2:20-21 NKJ) The sun shall turn to darkness and the moon to blood before the coming of the great and awesome day of the Lord. And whoever calls on the name of the Lord shall be saved. (Joel 2:11 NKJ) For the day of the Lord is very terrible; who can endure it?**

The shield of faith must be used every day. Renewing it daily will give you the strength to stand up against the plans of the evil one. When you combine prayer and praise with your shield of faith, this action will be what you will need. The word of God must be read daily. Taking in His words will help your faith to grow, but we must remember that faith doesn't save us. We are only saved by the grace of God. Faith is not the source, but is the way to believe in and see God's grace: to receive it because you were touched by God's calling.

When one's faith has no flavor, then it is useless and God will throw it away. He will destroy the person with weak faith. He is not pleased with someone who has such a faith. We read in **(Revelation 3:15-16 NKJ)** these words, **"I know your works, that you are neither cold nor hot. I wish you were cold or hot. So then, because you are lukewarm and neither cold nor hot, I will vomit you out of My mouth.** This doesn't seem such a pleasant thing to happen to someone of weak faith, but with sincere faith there is hope for the things that cannot be seen. **(Hebrews 11:1 NKJ) Now faith is the substance of things hoped for, the evidence of the things not seen.** With faith in the promises of God, and, when one's faith is anchored in the promise of eternal life, you will walk with Jesus, the Prince of Peace, in Heaven.

Before 2500 BC there lived a man named Noah. This man was a righteous man with obedience to Almighty God. God came to him and warned him that He was going to flood the world and destroy the wickedness of man. This warning was to spare Noah and his family because he had found favor with God. God ordered him to make an ark. It was to be made of gopher-wood, have three decks with many rooms, and was to be covered with pitch. **(Genesis 6:15 NKJ)The length of the arch shall be three hundred cubits, its width fifty cubits and its height thirty cubits.** Now, we know, that all the thousands of animals, birds, and reptiles upon this earth could not all fit in the arch, but we also know that God is capable of preserving His creation. **(Matthew 19:26 NKJ) But with God all things are possible.**

Noah probably couldn't even imagine what God was going to truly do, when He said that He was going to flood the earth. I don't think that his mind was capable of comprehending the amount of water that God would be sending. With his family safe inside the ark it began to be moved with the wind and rain upon the waves. Prayers and praises to God must have filled the air inside, because with faith and trust he moved forward to complete God's will. The people around him must have thought that he was crazy for building a boat in the desert, until the day God closed the door and the rain began to fall. Where would we be if Noah had faith and did not have the desire to move forward with works to fulfill God's will?

We need to believe in and rely on His strength as our Creator and believe that He will keep His promises He gave to us in His word, the Bible. He gives a promise of eternal life to those who have not seen but still believe and love the Lord. This belief is the most precious thing one could possess, and when we go through our trials with our hope in the Lord, His strength will help us through because of our faith in Him. With faith one will know that their soul will be saved on judgment day. **(John 20:29 NKJ) Jesus said to him, "Thomas, because you have seen me, you have believed. Blessed are those who have not seen and yet have believed."**

But how do we know that God is faithful? We must begin with the knowledge and wisdom that was written in His word. Here are a few verses in the Bible that speaks of His faithfulness and that we can trust in Him.

(1 Corinthians 1:9 NKJ) God is faithful, by whom you were called into the fellowship of His Son, Jesus Christ our Lord.

(2 Corinthians 1:18 NKJ) But as God is faithful--.

(1 Thessalonians 5:24 NKJ) He who calls you is faithful, who also will do it.

(Hebrews 2:17 NKJ) Therefore, in all things He had to be made like His brethren that He might be a merciful and faithful High Priest in the things pertaining to God, to make propitiation for the sins of the people.

(1 John 1:9 NKJ) If we confess our sins, He is faithful and just to forgive us our sins and cleanse us from all unrighteousness.

In His word it also tells of what is in the center of His being; His essence of who He truly is. He is love that is perfect, pure and never ending. *(1John 4:7-11 NKJ) Beloved, let us love one another, for the love of God; and everyone who loves is born of God and knows God. He who does not love does not know God, for God is love. In this the love of God was manifested toward us, that God has sent His only begotten Son into the world, that we might live through Him. In this is love, not that we loved God, but that He loved us and sent His Son to be the propitiation for our sins. Beloved, if God so loved us, we ought to love one another.*

This is His eternal promise. He will always love us and we can count on that love because it comes from the heart and mind of God; a love that does not waver. He is also described as the Father of Lights who does not change or rethink His plan He put into motion. We can read this in *(James 1:17 NKJ) Every good gift and every perfect gift is from above and comes from the Father of lights, with whom there is no variation or shadow of turning.* This is the light that lights up the darkness of this world and exposes the sins of the heart with God's eternal heavenly light.

Have you checked your faith lately?

1. Do you believe that Jesus is truly the Son of God?   -Yes   No
2. Do you believe that He died to save you?   -Yes   No
3. Do you believe that His blood was spilled to wash away your sins?   -Yes   No
4. Do you believe that He rose from His grave and sits at the right hand of God?   -Yes   No
5. Do you believe that God can see into your hearts desires?   -Yes   No
6. Do you believe that all things are under His feet?   -Yes   No
7. Do you believe that heaven is real?   -Yes   No
8. Do you believe that Jesus is coming back to wipe away all sin?   -Yes   No
9. Do you long to be surrounded with the love of God that is up in heaven?   -Yes   No

If you answered yes to every question then you are truly blessed, but check your heart because God can see into all the hidden places. There is nothing that can be hidden from Him. Christian or non-Christian; all things will be exposed.

CHAPTER TWO

Simple Faith

When we simplify our faith in God our faith and trust in Him will grow. Trust is the key word here. If there is no true trust in Him then the mind will be clouded with worry and questions. How does one let go and put faith in the loving Father in heaven, believing that He has everything in control?

We should begin with the knowledge and believe that we are His children and He is our loving Father. God understands our weaknesses and sees past our flaws. He longs to be close to His children, and as with any loving father He will take care of His children. A father provides for his children's needs and all their hearts desires, if it is a good thing. With wisdom comes understanding and looking beyond a child's way of thinking. He will protect them from harm and guide with a loving and firm hand. God is the ultimate Father. He will provide for our daily needs and He will fulfill the desire of the heart, if it is lined up with His will. His word is filled with heaven's wisdom and is beyond the way His children can truly understand and think.

We must see God as our "complete need". He should be seen as our Comforter, Healer, Protector, and Provider. He is the way to receive rest from this crazy world. When we look at Him as our Comforter, what should we see? We should see and believe that His eyes and ears are open to those who love Him. **(Psalms 34:15 NKJ) The eyes of the Lord are upon the righteous and His ears are open to their cry.** The key word in this Bible verse is, **<u>righteous,</u>** those who live a godly life under His eyes. He will not give comfort to those who live with the world in their hearts, but I feel that He will help those who He knows who will turn to Him later in their lives. He will give comfort in our hour of need. **(Isaiah 66:13 NKJ) As one whom his mother comforts, so will I comfort to you.** This is a promise that God will be with all who love Him and are going through loss, sorrow, disappointments and frustrations. **(Psalms 34:17-18 NKJ) The righteous cry out and the Lord hears and delivers them out of all their troubles. The Lord is near to those who have a broken heart and saves such as have a contrite spirit.** God sent the Comforter, the Holy Spirit, to be with us in our daily lives –to give strength to the weak, hope for the heart, and guide us through the darkness of this world. The Holy Spirit is the power of God with us, and no one can say the Lord is Lord without the Comforter (Holy Spirit) being with them. **(1 Corinthians 12:3 NKJ)–no one can say that Jesus is Lord except by the Holy Spirit.**

As I have said before, Jesus came to heal the body and soul. His touch healed every type of disease in the land of Israel as He walked among the Israelites and Gentiles. There is no reason not to believe that He isn't still a healer of bodies today because God is still in the miracle business. We must believe this and hold onto the hand of God. He may not heal one instantly but I believe that He can do this if that is His choice to do so. He will guide one to the wisdom that is needed to heal the body if we were to ask in prayer for help. **(Psalms 103:3 NKJ) who forgives all your iniquities, who heals all your diseases.** He will put the doctors in your path that can help you. One of my favorite verses in God's word is (**Romans 8:31-32 NKJ: If God is for us, who can be against us? He who did not spare His own son, but delivered Him up for us all, how shall He not with Him also freely give us all things?** Helping us with **all** things, not just some, but **all**! We need to look past our way of thinking that is filled with doubts and stop putting limits on what God can do for the individual! We should see Him as our healer of the body, healer of the broken hearts and healer of the wounded souls. He is our heavenly Father that cares deeply for His children.

When we trust God we can believe that we are under His protective wings, just as David stood up against Goliath with faith and God by his side. As the story goes a Philistine challenged the armies of Israel to send out their best warrior to stand up against him. This man was a giant of nine feet tall with a sword, with a spear and with a javelin. But David came with the Lord by his side and the God of the armies of Israel behind him; even though the Israelites were terrified of this giant of a man. David had faith that God would deliver this Philistine into his hands. He faced this man with a sling and five smooth stones. He placed a stone in his sling pouch and hurled the stone through the air hitting the giant on his forehead, causing him to fall down. And he used the man's own sword to cut off his head. He had won the battle because God was by his side. So can we trust that He is by our side when we face our giants in our personal battles? Can we look toward God for strength with a belief that He will never leave our side? We must put our trust in our loving Father to be our protector. **(Psalms 36:7 NKJ) How precious is your loving kindness, O God! Therefore the children of men put their trust under the shadow of your wings.**

We can never know how many times God has protected us without realizing it but those who believe in God's protection will know when God stepped in and kept them from harm. I believe in divine intervention because I will never forget the times God protected me and there was no doubt in my mind that He did.

One I was going on a half hour trip to another town to pick up my grandchildren. I remember being tired and turning off the main road and driving the side road to my daughter's house. I have to admit I was driving on the double yellow line, which means couldn't see other cars coming. Before I got to the top of the hill a small voice told me, "Move over," so I did. Less than five seconds later a young driver flew passed me doing the same thing, driving on the yellow line. If I hadn't obeyed the Holy Spirits leading we would have hit each other at forty five miles an hour. There was a very good possibility that the young driver would have been killed because my car was heavier and larger than his little truck. God not only protected me, He also protected that young driver, and besides who knows but God what He has planned in the years ahead for both of us.

Years ago I worked at an Assisted Living Facility in the evening cooking for the residents. Usually I would gather up my coat and keys to go home at the end of my shift. One evening I was walking down the hall that led to the back where my car was parked. Half way down the hall a loud voice came into my head that said, "Don't go that way." It was so loud that my hands went up into the air and it felt like my feet lifted slightly up off the ground. This put the brakes on with a screech you might say and then I told the Lord, "Ok Lord, let's go out the front door." What was out there I don't know, but I believe that was God's hand had protected me from harm or even death.

God protects His children. He gives His angels charge over us. **(Psalms 91:9-11 NKJ) Because you have made the Lord, who is my refuge, even the Most High, your dwelling place. No evil shall befall you, nor shall any plague come near your dwelling; for He shall give His angels charge over you, to keep you in all your ways.** We have to believe in the strength, guidance, and the loving care of the Father in heaven, with a belief in His ability to protect us as long as we live a godly life before Him. **(Psalms 121:8 NKJ) The Lord shall preserve you're going out, and you're coming in from this time forth and forevermore.**

God is our provider because this earth we live on is God-given and made to provide for our needs. **(Genesis 1:29-30 NKJ) And God said, "See, I have given you every herb that yields seeds which is on the face of the earth and every tree whose fruit yields seeds; it shall be food for you. Also, every beast of the earth, to every bird in the air, and everything that creeps on the earth, in which there is life, I have given every green herb for food", and it was so.** The tree alone is used for many things. It provides wood for heat, wood for building our homes, and shade for the summertime. It makes oxygen and produces food and we are provided with life giving water. All these things are what we need to survive, but when it comes to our wants and needs we need to recognize what is essential and what is a desire. We need shoes for our feet, but do we need the latest fashion? Should we expect God to provide this? We need a reliable car, but do we need a Lamborghini; a car that is the price of a large and very expensive home?

God know our needs and is willing to fulfill our hearts desire, **if this desire is lined up with His will**. We need to realize that His plan He put together will be fulfilled- the plan of eternal life with Him. The destruction of all sin will soon come to be, and no one will be able to stop Him.

We need to stop looking up to God only with our hands held out to receive our desires and wants. Our hands should be raised up in praise and worship more than opened to receive. He can give beyond what we ask for, but in His wisdom He knows if it is a wise to give us everything we ask for. He can see into our future and knows if it would be the right thing for the individual. He knows that if someone were to win the lottery then their need for Him may fade away. Money can easily take the place of the loving Father in heaven. In the news I saw this happen to a successful singer. She started out serving the Lord with her amazing voice but got caught up with money and drugs and it destroyed her; if she had kept her focus on God and serving Him with the talents He gave her she would still be alive to give God glory. It is all about choice isn't it and keeping God first in ones lives. When we pray for something we need to remember these words, "**If it be your will, Lord**." These words when spoken will reveal what is in the heart. The heart is saying I surrender to the Almighty God and recognize His sovereignty as my Lord in my life. He is above all things. We have to believe that He will provide our needs and our heart's desire if it will further His kingdom.

> **(Matthew 6:33 NKJ) "But seek first the kingdom of God and His righteousness and all these things shall be added to you."**

What do you think the key words are in this verse? They are: **seek first the kingdom of God and His righteousness.** One must put God first in their life- there is no way around this. It will be hard to walk on the narrow way to eternal life with one foot on the wide path that leads to destruction. It will be impossible to please God if we cannot step away from this world.

> **(Philippians 4:6, 19 NKJ) Be anxious for nothing, but in everything by prayer and supplication**

with thanksgiving, let your request be known to God---And my God shall supply all your needs according to His riches in glory by Jesus Christ.

What are the key words in these verses? They are: **be anxious for nothing---and my God shall supply all your needs.** We are worriers and find it hard to completely trust God to fulfill our needs. To have complete faith without any doubts we need to step away from the mirror with the question, "What can I do?" Stop looking to yourself for the answer and look up to heaven for guidance, because when we trust in God we then have confidence in Him. When we have confidence in His ability to do all things, our confidence in ourselves will grow because we believe that He is leading the way. We can trust in the loving Father, and that in itself is another miracle.

CHAPTER THREE

Clean Your Spiritual Heart

In order for our faith to grow with trust in the Lord, we must clean our spiritual hearts, to feel the presence of God in our daily lives. All the negativity one carries can block the flow of peace and contentment to the believer's heart, and when this happens we cannot be fruitful in our walk of faith.

How does one let the anger, non-forgiveness, and hurt leave the mind? Begin by seeing that what you are doing is not pleasing to the Lord. Did Jesus not teach that the non-forgiving person will not be forgiven of their sins, if they refuse to forgive? **(Colossians 3: 12–14 NKJ) Therefore as the elect of God, holy and beloved, put on tender mercies, kindness, humility, meekness, longsuffering; bearing with one another and forgiving one another, if anyone has a complaint against another; even as Christ forgave you, so you also must do. But above all these things put on LOVE, which is the bond of perfection.** We need to forgive the person that caused us pain and pray for them, and if there is an opportunity to bless them then we need to do so. By doing this an enemy may well become a friend, or at least soften the heart of the one that is against you. Maybe they would even come and ask for forgiveness for the hurt and trouble they caused you, but one must be willing to forgive if this should happen, and ask God to forgive us for the sin of the non-forgiving heart. We need to have God's help so we can forgive others, especially when the hurt and anger run deep. We have to forgive them even if they never change their feelings about us.

What do we do when we see someone who says there is no need for forgiveness and so refuses to do so? We must realize that it is the individual's choice to forgive or not, but when we are blinded to the truth in God's word we will not be able to see the importance of forgiveness. The unforgiving heart will be robbed of the blessings that come from heaven, which is good health and receiving answers to the prayers, when we humble the heart before the Lord. If one still holds resentment for the person who caused problems for you or, someone that is close to you, or has any other reason not to forgive, it will keep the Holy Spirit from moving in one's life, because we are grieving the Holy Spirit. **(Ephesians 4:30 NKJ) And do not grieve the Holy Spirit of God, by whom you we sealed for the day of redemption.**

What does it mean when we do this? First let's look at the meaning of the word grieve. The American Heritage Dictionary gives us the meaning, "to cause to be sorrowful; distress," So what is causing the Holy Spirit to feel this way? It is all sin. He yearns for all to live a godly life because He knows that those who do not turn from sin will not inherit eternal peace. The only way to stop this is to be reconciled with the Lord, through repentance with a completely new attitude toward God. Because of our sinful nature we all still fall short of giving God glory, but we are sealed with Holy Spirit of promise, when we accept Jesus as Lord and King. **(Ephesians 1:13-14 NKJ) In Him you also trusted, after you heard the word of truth, the gospel of your salvation; in which also, having believed, you were sealed with the Holy Spirit of promise.** This is our eternal blessing.

So if we had to carry all our negative emotions around like suitcases then what would it be like? Let's start by picking all of them up. We will begin with **anger** and **hate**. These two suitcases can be pretty heavy. Do you feel the weight pulling on your heart and soul right now? But you are not done. You need to pick up **vengeance, non-forgiveness, worry, anxiety, pride, depression** and **fear**. Now you are really struggling to carry all the bags. Are you refusing to let go and too prideful to ask for help with such a load? **(Matthew 11: 28-30 NKJ) "Come to me, all you who labor and are heavy laden, and I**

will give you rest. Take up my yoke upon you and learn from me, for I am gentle and lowly in heart and you will find rest for your souls; for my yoke is easy and my burden is light. Many claim to be a Christian but are still carrying excess baggage. Why? It is because we cannot seem to trust completely in the loving Father? Or maybe we don't want to let go because one's feelings are being justified in their mind. Do we keep walking toward Heaven feeling like a true Christian, but live in denial of our weak faith or sins? We approach Heaven's pearly gates for the final prize, to receive our reward, but we will find out that it is too narrow for us to walk through with all those bags. Sadly, many refuse to drop any. What is more important; our self-made burdens we carry or eternal peace in heaven? Realize also, that none of these negative emotions will be allowed to cross over into God's home. We have to let them go because His home is perfect and free of sin and we cannot enter with all of this in our hearts. He will not let any of this touch His holy ground. This sounds to me like paradise is waiting for those who believe and are longing for, the ones who have a forgiving heart.

No matter how hard things are for us we need to let go and reach for the strength that is eternal. We need to run to the name of the Lord, our Towering Fortress, and give everything to Him. By placing this in His hands we can find peace among our earthy burdens. It may take a while to let go, because God wants us to see clearly why we are holding on so tightly to our self-made burdens. We can only grow in our faith if we let God do some trimming in our lives, and help us learn from our mistakes. Once we humble our self and see what kind of sinner we truly are, then we can begin to drop our suitcases, one at a time. This will help us to stand up straight because our burdens will become lighter, and then we can step through Heaven's gate to receive that wonderful gift from the loving Father. Letting go of this world with Jesus in your sight will reveal what is truly important.

Dangerous Ground

When your frustrations turn to anger
You are walking on dangerous ground-
For there your heart is hardened
And grace will not be found-

The mind will be filled with questions;
Your behavior you will justify-
Beware of the quicksand you are on,
For the evil one is by your side-

Turn from the thoughts that are blinding you;
Turn to the truth; from above given-
Forgive the one standing before you,
Step back onto solid ground to be forgiven.

CHAPTER FOUR

Believe and Receive

Trusting in the love of God is a must in one's believe and faith. God is eternal, therefore His love is eternal. And since it is never ending, we should believe in this everlasting and wonderful love. We need to hold onto this love that came from Heaven (Jesus,) because if it weren't for love we would not be here. If it weren't for love we would not be forgiven of our sins. If it weren't for love we would not have the promise of eternal peace in Heaven. Love is our greatest gift that came to save us. He gave us life so we could love, serve, and worship Him. Our loving Father deserves more than what we are capable of giving Him, but I know He desires life for all of His children.

Faith knows that God can do all things with the heart and mind filled with knowledge that He will answer prayers. Believe and receive. Receive and be relieved. There is no other way to receive peace from Him without trusting in Him. With the world in such disorder around us it is hard to keep our faith strong. That is why it is important to renew the mind and heart daily by refreshing the spirit with prayer, praising, and God's word. The power of Heaven is released when we praise God in the good times and the bad times. Keeping the heart merry with songs going up to the Lord will fill the space, where ever one may be at that moment in time. His presence and His strength will be with us for the bad times that are ahead, and with life there will always be hard times we have to go through. They are the storms of life.

Many feel that God is so far in outer-space that He seems unreachable. Their minds are filled with how the world thinks and believes. Yes,

I know that we can never fathom the true greatness of God, but we should be able to see His presence everywhere. **(James 4:8 NKJ)** says how to get close to Him…**therefore submit to God. Resist the devil and he will flee from you. Draw near to God and He will draw near to you. Cleanse your hands you sinners; and purify your hearts, you double minded. Lament and mourn and weep! Let your laughter be turned to mourning and your joy to gloom. Humble yourselves in the sight of the Lord and He will lift you up.**

The first thing one must do is submit to God. Surrender all that you are and all that you will be to Him. Then He will come to you and your life will never be the same again. Turn from all sin and the Devil will run away, but he will try every day to make you fail in your renewed life. That is why we need to put on the armor of God **(Ephesians 6: 10-17 NKJ)** on daily to battle against the evil one. When you surrender to God He will lift you out of the darkness that you were in and His light will forever shine in your heart.

So let us begin by believing that God's presence is truly all around us. **(Deuteronomy 4:39 NKJ) Therefore know this day and consider it in your heart that the Lord himself is God in heaven above and on the earth beneath; there is no other.** We need to have faith that He is behind us as a rear guard, keeping watch that nothing can slip up behind us and conquer us, and trusting that His power and presence will protect us in all situations. If we see God as only looking down upon us and never being by our side or living in our hearts, we are putting limits on what God can do. Get rid of the doubts by believing in His eternal power and greatness. Pray that He will help you see the truth. He is our greatest supporter. He is our refuge from the darkness of this world. We can trust we can be safe in His hands, even when we are going through persecution, because of our faith and love for Him.

Picture this in your mind: When we kneel before God in prayer and worship we are resting upon His hand. We are high above the black swirls of the sin of the world that is now below us. You look down and see disfigured faces of anger and sadness with arms and hands trying to stay above it all-to catch a breath of relief. Thousands of souls are being drained of the life that is God-given. We are His children and can have a personal relationship at His right hand. Having fellowship with the Lord is an honor and privilege, because we are all such sinners who fall short daily of giving God glory and do not deserve the blessings He gives to us: forgiveness, grace and love. **(Romans 3:23 NKJ) for all have sinned and fall short of the glory of God.**

As we walk through this valley of life there will be many obstacles that we must face. Our faith and God's word will surround us like a shield. It will be like walls of mountains will be our protection. We will still have to go through tough times, but we must believe in God's strength to be there to help us through them. **(Matthew 28:20 NKJ) "...lo, I am with you always, even unto the end of the world."** As we move forward through the storms we can have hope in the Lord to go before us to clear the way. When we go through life's struggles we must understand that there is a reason why. We may not see the reason at first, but in the end the truth will be revealed, and God can use all situations that we go through to help others in their struggles. He can live within the heart as our Comforter and be the one who will dry the tears, heal the broken hearts, and strengthen the soul.

And I know Christians do fall victim to the hands of madness and their life is taken from them. We may not understand why God does not prevent this from happening, but we just have to leave that in His hands and keep trusting in Him. If we keep trying to find the answer to that we will be opening up the thought, if God is love how could He let this happen. Then you will become discouraged and your faith will fade.

CHAPTER FIVE

Rely on His Guidance

God can use anything to reveal His presence in one's life. He revealed Himself to me while I was looking for a place to park my car so I could go into a local book store. I came up to a light waiting to turn green and was hoping that I would get a spot that was close. I drove through the intersection and had to stop because someone decided to parallel-park; but all of a sudden they changed their mind and moved on. As I drove forward a small voice said, "**You will park here**." I heard this, obeyed and parked in that spot. One might say so what, but I don't like to parallel-park because it takes me too long. What I am trying to tell you is this: it was like someone else was driving and backed into the parking space, just like a pro. It was the Holy Spirit driving the car for me. There were no thoughts of "Could I do this?" or, "Should I try this spot?" There no doubts at all. My loving Father revealed to me that He will be the confidence I need to fulfill His will for me. After all, why should we worry about His plans for us? All of His plans were made in Heaven, and all of those plans are for our good and will help fulfill His will.

Our Creator, our loving Father, guides those who rely on Him completely, even those who sometimes struggle with their faith. It may be that all have that problem once in a while. We are people that are far from perfect and may have days with doubts about our faith. If there are some who say they have no doubts and are telling the truth, then they are truly blessed. What a blessing it would be to completely trust in God for all things-to trust in Him to supply ones daily needs and to lead the way. To look past ones doubts and keeping hope alive with faith anchored in the rock of our salvation. **(Romans 8:32 NKJ) He who did not spare His own Son, but delivered Him up for us all, how shall He not with Him also give us all things?** This verse tells of God's amazing love for all of us and His generosity and willingness to give to His children what they ask for.

God's hand is there for our guidance, which is His Holy spirit who is filled with power from Heaven. This gift was sent to us so that we would not be alone-so we can receive comfort and strength. **(Proverbs 3:5 NKJ)** tells us to trust in God with all our heart…**Trust in the Lord with all your heart and lean not on your own understanding.** Trusting in Him to know what is best for us is important because when we start following our own thoughts, that is, trying to figure out our own problems without asking for His help, we will find out that we could be bringing in more struggles. When we acknowledge our need for Him He will guide the way we should go. **(Proverbs 3:6 NKJ) In all your ways acknowledge Him, and He shall direct your paths.)** Relying on Him for guidance is the only way to keep on the narrow path that leads to eternity with Jesus.

What are some of the things that will keep one from trusting in God's strength and guidance? Doubt is a big one. When we doubt we stop Him from giving guidance because our faith is lukewarm. It will break the flow or connection that comes from Heaven. Doubt in the mind and heart is from Satan, the ruler of this world, and when we become angry toward God for not answering a prayer we have become darkened by evilness. Sometimes our motives for receiving an answer to a request may not be truthful before God. You may try to hide or lie about your true motive before God, but there is no hiding anything from Him. The night sky is like the brightness of the noon day to Him. We are impatient also when it comes to wanting our prayers to be answered, but He is never late when it comes to answering prayers. He knows the right time when He should answer our prayers, or when to not answer at all, because what we want may be not the right thing for us. We have to remember that everything God does is done to further His kingdom. His plans will not be stopped by anyone or anything. The non-forgiving heart will also stop one from receiving guidance. All of this is not pleasing to the loving Father in Heaven-the one who sent His Son because He desires all to be saved, and when we are forgiven and believe that we are, but still bring up guilt of a past sin, this will also cause prayers not to be answered. God forgets the sins He has forgiven. Shouldn't we move on and forget them also?

CHAPTER SIX

Believe in His wonderful love

We need to hold onto His love like it is the only way one can make it to Heaven, like it is the only way to survive this insane world, and like it is the only way to walk someday with Jesus. It is and is our greatest gift that came from the Father in Heaven. Do you believe this? I certainly do and there is no way I could keep going if it weren't for His love for me.

Love is a powerful emotion. If all were to love others as God commands this world would be totally different than it is right now. His love can change just one heart or, the entire world. **(John 15:9-13 NKJ) "As the Father loved me, I also have loved you; abide in my love. If you keep my commandments, you abide in my love, just as I keep my Father's commandments and abide in His love. These things I have spoken to you, that my joy may remain in you and that your joy may be full. This is my commandment, that you love one another as I have loved you. Greater love has no one than this, than to lay down one's life for his friends.** Jesus was telling His disciples the importance of loving others and it was Heaven's love that was leading Him to the cross. His death on the cross was His Father's plan to save His children. Since He put our needs first (the need for a Savior), then we should put the needs of others before one's own needs-to make sacrifices that will give honor to the Father in Heaven, and to be willing to go that extra mile to further God's kingdom.

I have mentioned this verse before, but I feel writing about it can never be overdone. It is **(John 3:16 NKJ), For God so loved the world, that He gave His only begotten Son, that whoever believes in Him should not perish but have everlasting life.** To me this is the center of the Bible-the heartbeat of God. It's the reason we are here. Compassion, caring, and the sovereignty of our Creator are woven throughout these words. His longing for His children to turn from their sinful lives and come willingly to Him with a repenting heart is very apparent. Why would anyone not want to live with this love in their lives? Why are people in such denial about the reality of God? Why do people get so offended when someone talks about God? Why would one not want their life to become easier through His strength that is in His love? As I heard a nine year old girl say, "Why can't people just believe in God? That would put an end to all this stuff."

Yes indeed, why can't everyone just love God? As a Christian the answer to this has many reasons. The first one is that many cannot comprehend or look past their own doubt in the existence in something that is all powerful, all knowing, and above all things. That is what God is. People don't want to see anything as sin because sinful choices are due to a lustful heart. Sin is appealing, self-satisfying, and just plain fun for those who don't believe. They feel that they have the right to have fun, and what is wrong with that? Oh my, how shall I answer that one? **(John 4:15) If you love the Father in heaven you will keep His commandments.** The keys words are **"Love the Father."** When we love God these desires will fade away and the truth will live in the heart. His love can save the soul and bring peace to the heart. It can open up new opportunities for a new life that will help one walk the narrow way to Heaven. To believe in His wonderful love will help release the burdens of life, and the burdens will become lighter because Jesus will be carrying them for you. Many feel that God could never love them because of the things they have done- because of the guilt they carry. This is another reason why people don't turn to God. They believe in this lie of the devil. He has convinced them it is the true. They are blinded by the darkness of this world, but God's love-His loving light- can penetrate all darkness, and His love is a gift for all and will never change because it goes to eternity.

(1 Corinthians 4:5 NKJ) Therefore judge nothing before the time, until the Lord comes, who will both bring to light the hidden things of darkness and reveal the counsels of the hearts. Then each one's praise will come from God.

(John 3:20 NKJ) For everyone that practicing evil hates the light and does not come into the light, lest their deeds should be exposed. But he who does the truth comes into the light, that his deeds may be clearly seen, that they have been done in God.

(Ephesians 5:8 NKJ) For, you were once darkness but now you are light in the Lord. Walk as children of light...

Once we accept and truly believe in the Fathers love then we can walk daily in His presence. We can rest in the reassurance that He will take care of us and that He will protect us and help us through life's storms. He will give comfort in the time of loss or disappointment. **(Psalms 37:23, 24 NKJ) The steps of a good man are ordered by the Lord, and He delights in his way. Though he falls, he shall not be utterly cast down; for the Lord upholds him with His hand.** With love surrounding us we will learn to be still before Him, so we can hear that small voice leading the way. **(Isaiah 30:21 NKJ) Your ears shall hear a word behind you, saying "This is the way, walk in it," whenever you turn to the right hand or whenever you turn to the left.**

CHAPTER SEVEN

Live with eternal hope

D id you know that hope is a gift from God, just as faith is a gift? They are woven together with God's love and cannot be separated. God's eternal hope for men (Jesus) came from Heaven with an obedient heart and love for all. Without this hope there would be no hope for our future. Without this hope we would all be orphans with no chance of being adopted. Forever we would have a longing- a need that would never be fulfilled. For if you have no hope you have no faith, and if you have no faith you have no hope. These two are united with God. You cannot have one without the other.

So as we walk daily upon this God given earth we need to live with eternal hope filling our minds and hearts. The blood of Jesus was spilled for all mankind. He was, and is, our only eternal hope. There is no other name in Heaven or on earth that can free us from the sins of this world. He is the atonement for our sins and the only one that can cover our sins or erase our misdeeds. Through this act upon the cross, we were shown the only way to eternal life. **(Leviticus 17:11 KJ) For, the life of the flesh is in the blood, and I have given it to you upon the altar to make atonement for your souls; for it is the blood that makes atonement for the soul. (Romans 5:11 KJ) And not only so, but we also joy in God through our Lord Jesus Christ, by whom we have now received the atonement.**

He is our salvation to be born again into a new person with a heart that has been changed and saved from eternal damnation. It was the only way to save God's children. It was the perfect plan that was made in

Heaven, and anything that comes from heaven has a purpose- to fulfill the heavenly Fathers will. He wants His lost sheep (His children) to be with Him in Heaven and be free of earthly burdens so we can walk by His side with His peace. **(John 3:3 NKJ) Most assuredly, I say to you, unless a man is born again, he cannot see the kingdom of God.** Unless we repent and accept Jesus as one's Savior and the sovereignty of His Father we will not enter God's kingdom. We must turn from the sins of this world and follow the way Jesus (our eternal hope leads to be able to go to Heaven. We must be willing to let God change the hidden person inside. **(John 3:17 NKJ) For, God did not send His Son into the world to condemn the world, but that the world through Him might be saved. (Acts 4:12 NKJ) Nor is there salvation in any other name under heaven given among men by which we must be saved.**

We have a heavenly lawyer who will speak for all who accept Him as their Lord and His guidance. We are now acquitted of our guilt and sin. Therefore, we are **justified through His blood upon the cross**. For only Jesus the Son of God is capable of speaking for the changed heart, which chose the narrow way to paradise. How can one not be grateful for this? This is what love is-to speak for the worms that we are-looking past our faults, weaknesses and reaching out with the willingness to forgive all sins of the hearts and souls.

> **(Acts 13:38 KJ) Be it known unto you therefore, men and brethren, that though this man (Jesus) is preached unto you the forgiveness of sins. (Romans 5:9 KJ) Much more then, being justified by the blood, we shall be saved from wrath (judgment) through Him. (Acts 13:39 KJ) And by Him all that believe are justified from all things, from which ye could not be justified by the laws of Moses.**

Can you not see now how important it was for God to send His Son to save His children? There was no other way under Heaven to accomplish this. This alone should humble the heart in all of us. This alone should cause us to raise our arms up in worship to the loving Father and bow our hearts by touching our faces to the soil of this earth.

Through this covenant and promise from God our life is paid in full- taking us away from the power of sin and death. All things are below the feet of Jesus, our Lord and King. The darkness of this world will never have any control over Him, for even the demons tremble at the mention of His name. **(James 2: 19 NKJ) You believe that there is one God. You do well. Even the demons believe and tremble.** Through **redemption** we are saved from fiery judgment. We are saved to walk into paradise and to walk by our God with no more of the sin that lives in the heart and mind ever again. I will say that again, "no more shall sin live in the heart and mind again!"

When we accept Jesus as Lord in our life we become **sanctified** through His blood. We are living in this **sanctification** day by day. God has set us apart from the world to be forever with Him-to be partakers of the heavenly joy and hope- to be His children that have come home from their wondering ways. We are now holy before God's eyes and now have the responsibility to live a Godly life, what He desires all of us to do. **(Hebrews 10:10, 14 NKJ) By that will we have been sanctified through the offering of the body of Jesus Christ once and for all, for by one offering (His death upon the cross) He was perfected forever those who are being sanctified. (1 Corinthians 1:30 NKJ) But of Him you are in Christ Jesus, who became for us wisdom from God-and righteousness-and sanctification-and redemption.**

Through the **righteousness** of Christ Jesus, the Son of God, we are standing right with God. We were once facing the darkness of this world but now we have turned to the light that leads to Heaven. We have turned to the truth that will someday free us from this sinful world. The **righteousness** of God can shine upon our faces and be a beacon for others to be saved. We are each a lighthouse that guides the wayward traveler safe to the shores of God's presence, away from the black seas of eternal darkness. **(Romans 3:25 KJ) Whom God hath set forth to be the propitiation through faith in his blood, to declare his righteousness for the remissions of sins that are the past, through the forbearance of God.**

When we have an attitude of gratitude that comes from repentance of one's sins, then we will see God in another light. Our hostility toward God and others will change and when it comes you will learn to love God and others, because then you will want to have fellowship with your Lord and Maker. Pleasing God will become your number one priority. Being reconciled through the spilling of the Lord's blood will save your soul and spirit. **(Colossians 1: 20-23 NKJ***), By Him, to reconcile all things to Himself, by Himself, whether things on earth or things in heaven having made peace through the blood of His cross. And you, who once were alienated and enemies in your mind by wicked works, yet now He has reconciled in the body of His flesh through death, to present you holy and blameless and above reproach in His sight-if indeed you continue in the faith, grounded and steadfast, and are not moved away from the hope of the gospel which you heard, which was preached to every creature under heaven, of which I, Paul, became a minister.***

Through the selfless act upon the cross Jesus went willingly to save us and be obedient to the Father in Heaven. This sacrifice can overcome all things. It gives us power to overcome the evil one's schemes. It overpowers his desire to destroy us. It is our right as children of God to pray through the blood of Jesus-the Lamb of God. Therefore, we can use it as a shield and weapon to protect ourselves. **(Revelation 12:11 KJ) And they overcame him by the blood of the Lamb and by the word of their testimony; and they loved not their lives unto the death.** In this scripture the word "**(they)**" is referring to Christians. It is telling us that we can overcome the devil through the blood of Jesus. We can put the armor of God on to withstand the plans of the devil, but it also says "**(the word of their testimony)**" meaning that we need to use the word of God like a sword to put up a good fight-to swing it back and forth with all ones might; cutting down all the weeds and thistles that are trying to stop you from moving forward to fulfill God's will. Let us never forget that is it God's strength that is in the sword you have in your hands. One cannot defeat the darkness of this world without the Holy Spirit living within the heart.

There is freedom through Jesus. He is the only one who sets men free from their sins. The power of darkness is broken because God's power is greater and will always be. Jesus is our deliverer from the captivity of a sinful lifestyle. This freedom is filled with hope in the Lord and we can dwell in the land of eternal liberty as we walk to Heaven's stairs. **(Romans 8:1-2 NKJ) there is therefore now no condemnation to those who are in Christ Jesus, who do not walk according to the flesh, but according to the Spirit; for the law of the Spirit of life in Christ Jesus has made me free from the law of sin and death. (Corinthians 1:10 NKJ) who delivered us from so great a death and does deliver us; in whom we trust that He will still deliver us.**

Our debt and our guilt have been cancelled. The remission of our sins will be done with the repentance of the heart and through the blood of the Lamb. Forgiveness from God is a great blessing to the humbled heart. To be pardoned by the loving Father shows His tender mercy for His children.

Jesus is our eternal hope. He is our greatest need in this lost world. The blood of Jesus was given freely to God's sinful children. It was and is offered to all who walk upon this earth. He is our salvation, redemption, atonement, righteousness, justification, sanctification, and deliverer from the power of evil. Through Him there is forgiveness and freedom. There is no one greater.

CHAPTER EIGHT

All are flawed

Does simply going to church give you faith? Do you believe because you go to church you are saved? When you stand before God for judgment will you feel confident about the Lord letting you enter Heaven? The false belief of a building saving you is a tragedy. The act of walking through church doors will not secure your place in Heaven. The true church resides in the hearts of all of us. The children that come together in a building or among the trees to worship with a humble and obedient heart are what the Father in Heaven is searching for.

We should not take our salvation so lightly. We must be sure we are walking the narrow way that is pleasing to the Father in Heaven. Churches were built by the hands of men. They can be huge, holding hundreds of people with many voices singing in the choir, or they can be as small as one room. All are the same. All have flaws because they were started by one person leading the way, and that one is a sinner like the rest of us. Do we really need a building to worship God? Do we need to give our ten percent to keep the church open? Should the money we give from the heart take care of an electric bill, water bill, insurance, pastor's wages, etc., or should we use the money to help someone in need? Some churches cost millions to operate because they are immense cathedrals. How much of a building is needed to worship God? If the farmer gets on his knees before God in his field of wheat with blue sky over his head, and thanks Him for the blessing of a good crop, is that not the same as one kneeling in church to worship and give thanks? Are they both not placing their hearts before God?

The worship we send up to the Lord should not be saved for just one particular day. Worship and praise should be seven days a week. By beginning our day with prayer and praising Him for who He is - thanking Him for the gifts you receive every day- are we not worshiping before God? I feel that we do not know how to truly worship our loving Father. We have lost our way. We do not give Him enough glory and honor because many act like an angel for one day and a devil the rest of the week. As a Christian we need to reveal our love for our Creator to others through our lifestyle-to be good example of the living waters that comes from within. **(John 7:38 NKJ) "He who believes in me, as the Scripture has said, out of the heart will flow rivers of living waters.**

All churches have the same problem. They believe what they are teaching is right and all the teachings of others are wrong. How can one be right and all others be wrong? How can all be right? The interpretation of God's word can always be changed to suit one's way of thinking. The arrogant heart can become prideful because they feel their faith is great, making them feel they are one of God's true disciples. How many trust their Pastor's words completely and don't search for proof of what He says to be right? How many Pastors refuse to respond when confronted with what they are saying is wrong? We need to remember that all men and women are capable of sinning. So let us not forget to prove all things.

I don't worry about what waits for me in Heaven, because it will be better than this world. In fact, it will be **beyond better** than this world, and if I had to live under a rock because I wasn't fruitful enough for God it wouldn't bother me- just as long as I was with my Jesus and freed from this sinful world to walk in paradise surrounded by God's love. What more could one want? Why should we think we deserve a fancy mansion to live in? Besides, when God tells us about the mansions that are waiting for those who believe, how can we truly know what they are? We think as humans do when it comes to the word mansions: Buildings, castles, home, towers, etc. How does anyone know what God truly means? **(1 Corinthians 2:9 NJK) "Eyes have not seen,**

nor ear hear, nor have entered into the hearts of man the things which God has prepared for those who love Him. No one can think as God does.

Religion comes in many forms- from worshiping idols which are man-made to worshiping in a building that is man-made. "Religion" is a harsh word and to me it sounds so far away from the Father. The rules and rituals made by someone who felt a calling. They need to tell others that they should follow their ideas because they believed God has led them to start a new church. How many of these callings were not from God? How many false religions are out there? How many are teaching lies? How many have let the power of self-importance put them ahead of God? We can be so easily caught up in religion that we forget about humble faith–the faith of a child.

In the Bible it warns us that those who are false teachers will be judged more harshly and will be thrown into the lake of fire. **(Revelation 19:20 NKJ) Then the beast (devil) was captured, and with him the false prophets who worked signs in his presence, by which he deceived those who received the mark of the beast and those who worshiped his image. These two were cast alive into the lake of fire burning with brimstone. (Matthew 7:15 NKJ) Beware of false prophets, who come to you in sheep's clothing, but inwardly they are ravenous wolves.** Teaching the gospel is a big responsibility because it is done under God's watchful eyes. When one is leading others it must be done to give the Creator glory and have Heaven's truth at the center of the teaching. We cannot put our self upon a pedestal of self-importance. This is a strong warning from God to those who distort, or change His word for their own desires.

Church can still be an uplifting experience for many out there. It can still bring many into the family of God, and mend the broken and wounded hearts with the love of Jesus, our Lord and King. It is where one can have fellowship with other Christians, but we need to remember that it is just a structure- a building that has a roof over it. When Jesus comes all things that were made by men- including churches- will be wiped away from God's earth. **(Revelation 21:1 NKJ) Now I saw a**

new heaven and a new earth, for the first heaven and the first earth had passed away. And there was no more sea.

If you choose not to go to church there is nothing wrong with that, as long as you keep close to God and be obedient to Him in your walk of faith. However we need to hear encouraging words of faith from others in our times of struggle. We also need to have prayer from others for our needs, and we need to grow in our faith by witnessing to others what God has done for us. Walking alone in your faith will make the journey to Heaven lonely and more difficult, but when we see others in church that praise God one day and treat other wrong the next we could very easily walk away from our faith because of discouragement. We also need to remember that there is no one that is without sin. All have their own flaws and God said that very few will be truly walking on the narrow path to life. We are all capable of doing thing we regret, but through the gift of faith and God's strength we can become conquers over the darkness of this world. **(Romans 8:37 NJK) ....we are more than conquerors through Him that love us.**

One thing we must do is step away from religion and into simple faith for our loving God in Heaven. We must be that little child that holds their Father's hand and, feeling safe as we walk by His side. We must receive the love that is in His heart for us, and if a Pastor is teaching something that is not in God's word then run as fast as you can from that church, because it may make the difference if you go to Heaven or not. We need to see the seriousness of our choices when it comes to our salvation. We need to prove all things. **(Romans 12:2 NKJ) And do not be conformed to this world, but be transformed by renewing the mind, that you may prove what, is good and acceptable and perfect will of God.**

CHAPTER NINE

Salvation

Since God sees all that our heart has hidden or even exposed before others, should we not do what is right before Him? Should we not fear the living God that can destroy the body and soul? Should we not want to be obedient because He holds our life in His hands? It is His choice if we walk with Him in Heaven. Whether or not we receive the gift of eternal life is entirely up to Him. Let us not be fooled by our own thinking- God will expose all things. There will be many that think they will be walking through Heaven's door, but God will turn them away. **(Matthew 7:22 NKJ) Many will say to Me in that day, "Lord, Lord, have we not prophesied in Your name, cast out demons in Your name and done many wonders in Your name? "And then I will declare to them, "I never knew you; depart from Me, you who practiced lawlessness!"** Do you want to be that person? The thought of that should bring fear to the heart and a tear to the eye. We cannot deceive God our loving Father and Creator in any way, for He is omniscient-knowing all things. Meaning He sees all things.

We need to expose our heart to God willingly and let Him show the darkness that is hidden in us. We need to humble ourselves before our Maker. There is no other way to receive the gift of eternal life. No one will be rewarded for bad behavior or for being a good person without faith. Be warned, it will be hard to see the truth that He will show you. It will be hard to swallow the truth without God by your side. We cannot choke to death when we swallow the truth, but we will choke to death when we swallow the devil's lies. Shame will fill the soul, but take heart. He will also take the sin and shame away and help change the person that you hide inside, should you humble yourself with repentance.

We should rejoice in the fact that God loves such sinners, as we all are such sinners that He loved us before creation **(Jeremiah 1:5 NKJ) Before I formed you in the womb I knew you.** He is willing to forgive and to forget through His Grace, after repentance from the heart. Our faith should reflect the truth that came from Heaven, Jesus. We should be that light in the darkness that will help lead others to their salvation. We need to do a daily check of the heart to be sure we are not denying our inner sins.

Faith is the single word that can move the walls of doubt that surround the heart. The power of this word comes directly from God. It is filled with the Holy Spirit, which is God's eternal power. So why should we worry and fret so when we have hope in the Lord? Why do we let are minds slip away from God's ability to be able to do all things? It is because we are weak in the heart and soul. Our need for God and His strength and guidance is so clear to me. Let us stop putting limits on what God can do. His love for His children is shown every day by changing the heart of the sinner- by the willingness to forgive us, and when God says no to a prayer there is a reason behind it, and this reason will be revealed for the one to see.

I've always believed that for someone to believe in God and accept His sovereignty all it takes is just one glance toward Heaven and the seed faith would be planted. Then the Lord would water that seed with His living waters to make it begin to grow-to change the inner person that only God can see. So let us all work on receiving the eternal prize waiting in Heaven, and while we are still walking upon this God-given earth let who believe be fruitful for God and be the lights in this world of darkness because we have the gift of faith.

So is one's faith without works pleasing to God? You may not see the work you do for the Lord grow when you are still living but you must believe that what you write or what you do will be seen and read, therefore still being fruitful even after ones passing.

Planting
Seeds for
God's glory

Shining Stars

To those who follow the Lord
They are His shining stars-
With hearts that are filled with hope,
Believing that He is never far-

Sharing the love of God with others
Will bring rewards from Heaven-
There they will bask in the light of God
And never need to be forgiven.

The Humble Heart

The humble heart should know about you Lord,
To serve you one needs to have this yearning-
Having the humble spirit before the Creator,
Committing one's life to Him with praising-

We were bought for a price that leads to Him,
The only true light that leads us home-
Giving the promise of rest and peace for all,
Telling of Heaven and never leaving us alone.

The Light from Heaven

Heaven is reflected upon my tears
My joy and hope, for Jesus is near

Heaven is living close to me,
The wonder of it will I soon see-

Heaven sings of glory; the Holy Lamb,
The living word; our King the great I Am-

Heaven is eternity for those who believe,
Showing in the hearts that chooses to receive

Grains of Gold

God scatters grains of gold
Before sinful man-
The wise gather these precious grains
Fulfilling His plan-

Planting them in the soil of their heart,
Waiting for the rain-
God's life giving water will grow more faith
Our heavenly gain-

When, trials come to your field of faith
The Harvest is near-
Live with God's strength in the heart
And do not fear

Walls of Jericho

March around your walls of Jericho
Bring the stones of darkness down-
Shout to the Lord and give Him glory,
Submit with obedience and trust now-

For He did not give us the spirit of fear,
But of power, love and a sound mind-
He surrounds you with His Holy Spirit,
That is filled with love for mankind.

Heavenly Stairs

Look upon the Savior's face
And this world will grow dim-
Believe in His loving grace,
Reaching out with trust to Him-

What glory you will see,
Nothing on earth will compare-
For you will be eternally free
When, you climb Heaven's stairs.

The Path of Light

Faith must be there for all to see,
In the heart it must be found-
To walk in the presence of God
Upon His holy ground-

Faith without works is empty,
Not pleasing to the eyes of the Lord-
One must walk on the path of light
And live with His holy word

The Gift of Faith

Your faith is a gift
And it needs to grow-
Fulfilling God's will,
To let His love show-

Faith cannot be mere words
That one speaks-
It must have action
For this is what God seeks.

The Living Rock

In my field of faith I plant seeds of hope,
Peace, forgiveness and love-
I wait Lord, for your living waters
To rain down from above-

Each seed I plant will give glory to you,
To bring more sheep into the flock-
Pointing to Jesus; the Prince of peace and joy,
As I stand upon the living rock

Let My Light Shine

Be silent! Hold your tongue!
They say to me-
Don't show your faith,
Your belief in thee-

For they are offended
By the words they hear-
They reject them,
Not wanting God near-

But they cannot take
The joy that is in me-
For I see Jesus, the Son of God
Waiting in eternity-

The hope for Heaven fills me
With love in my heart-
For I believe when He said,
"From you I will never part"

Only a fool will say
There is no wonderful Creator-
All will stand before God,
Our heavenly Maker-

So let my light shine brighter
Each and every day-
To bring blessings to others,
Giving glory to Him each day

Let Your Faith Bloom

Let your bloom of faith
Stand out for all to see-
Do not hide your belief
That has set you free-

Touch others around you
With God's saving love-
Tell them about Jesus,
Who, came from above

The Crystal Sea

When the Lord takes me to Heaven
And there was no home for me-
I would be content with His love
And a peaceful eternity-

There I would be at eternal rest,
By the heavenly Crystal Sea-
There I would listen to angels sing
And Jesus would be with me.

Blessings from Heaven

What a blessing my Father
Has given to me-
To show others my faith and His love,
That has set this child free-

There is no greater joy or delight
When, I do God's will-
I hear Him calling softly to my heart
When, I am quiet and still-

The works that He began in my soul,
He will soon complete-
It will give Him glory; I will give Him honor,
Helping others to see-

For my longing and trust in Him grows stronger
Each and every day-
I am truly blessed with His life saving love,
Before Him, I shall forever pray

God Spoke

Leaves rustle in the trees
As the wind goes by;
Like the breathe of God,
For His presence is nigh

The world and its creation
Praise Him for His love;
All birds sing and the cooing
Of the morning dove

The redwood trees stand tall
And point up to Heaven;
They say this is the way
Your sins can be forgiven

Thunder and lightning declare
His power and glory;
The rain dances as it tells
Of God's creation story

The majestic mountains look down
On what had been done;
All things upon this world
Were created by God and His son

He Walked in Victory

Victory walked on this earth
In the form of a man-
The steps He took were His Father's,
To complete God's holy plan-

His healing hands touched many
As He went His way-
Transforming broken bodies;
Freeing soul's everyday-

The heart that beat in His chest
Was filled with love-
Revealing our the Father in Heaven,
Who, watches from above

My Vow

I will go where you say,
If you Lord, but lead the way-

I will complete your will,
As you teach me to be still-

I will be the light for others to see,
For you have set this one free-

I will rely on your strength above
And always believe in your gentle love.

Have You Heard?

Have you heard? God is all seeing; all knowing;
All powerful and His presence is everywhere-
Have you heard? God is love, merciful; full of grace
And forgiving; for you He does care-

Have you heard? God is our Creator; our Provider;
Our Protector; with healing power in His hands-
Have you heard? God is giving; our resting place
And has an eternal perfect plan-

Have you heard? That He sent His Son Jesus,
With a never ending love from above-
Have you heard? There is nothing that can separate
Us from His wonderful perfect love